10 Minute Truths

Mr. Richmond
Thank You!
5/9/09

Aaron Davis

10 Minute Truths

Quick Inspiration to Rejuvenate,
Refuel and Refocus Your Life

Aaron Davis

10 Minute Truths

Quick Inspiration to Rejuvenate, Refuel and Refocus Your Life

To order additional copies contact:

Aaron Davis Presentations, Inc.

PO Box 81711

Lincoln, NE 68501

1.800.474.8755

Printed in the United States of America

This book is dedicated to the woman who has been my rock, strength, and comfort. In good times and bad, she has sustained me, stood by my side and encouraged me to use every gift God has given me. She has been instrumental in teaching me the lessons found within this book. Our relationship started over ten years ago, while we were in college, and we have been talking, laughing, and crying together ever since. Brooke, I thank God daily, not only that you put up with such a crazy man, but more importantly, that you have given me so much -- spiritually, mentally, and emotionally. I love you, babe!

10 Minute Truths

Table of Contents

Chapter	Page
Your Days Are Limited	1
Selfishness is Counterproductive	3
Deciding Who You Are Is Key	4
Opportunity Knocks - Can You Answer?	6
Failure is an Integral Part of Life	8
Self-Talk Can Be Dangerous	10
People are our Most Important Resources	12
Your Environment Determines Your Destiny	14
Life is Going to Shake You Up	16
Wishing Alone Gets You Nowhere	18
The Past Can Ruin the Future	20
It's the Little Things That Can Get You	22
We Have Two Ears and One Mouth for a Reason	24
Fear and Faith Cannot Co-exist	27
Moments Make Up Our Lives	30
Your Definition of Success is the Only One that Matters	32
Life Ends When We Stop Learning	35
Reasons Must Be Strong	38
We Eventually Become Like Those We Spend Time With	39
Your Strengths are What Get You Through	41
Friends are Important Parts of Our Lives	44
Life is a Contact Sport	48
Your Never Know Unless You Ask	50
Life Can Get Messy	52
Your Dreams are up to You	54
Sometimes it's Reasonable to be Unreasonable	56

10 Minute Truths

Table of Contents

Chapter	Page
It's Impossible to Live a Good Life Without Integrity	58
You Can't Swim Very Far with Floaties On	61
Life is Too Short to Spend Forty Hours Doing Something You Hate	63
You Already Have What it Takes	65
Life is Full of Pain but it's also Full of Choices	67
You Can Learn a lot by Digging Post Holes	69
People Can Be Like Termites	71
Losers Don't Value Fundamentals	73
Sometimes You Will Want to Quit	76
We All Have 24 Hours in a Day	78
Two Natural Remedies: Laughter and Tears	80
It's Easy to Find Someone to Blame	82
Teamwork Always Gets You Further	85
Worry is a Poor Investment of Time	87
The Power of Words	89
Preparation is the Prerequsite of Any Great Endeavor	91
The Apostles Didn't Just Sit Around	93
Rejection Opens the Door to Unlimited Possibilities	95
Gratitude Improves Your Attitude	96
Look in the Mirror: There is Your Toughest Competitor	98
Be Different to Receive Different Results	99
Sincerity is a Sign of Strength	101
Serving Others Improves Your Life	102
The Most Important People You Can Honor are Your Parents	103
One Final Truth	105

Speaking Engagements

Aaron Davis delivers inspiring and thought-provoking presentations to thousands of individuals each year at meetings, conferences and major events! Contact him today to INSPIRE and IGNITE your next event!

Speaking Topics:
- *Inspiration*
- *Sales & Service Success*
- *Leadership*
- *Team Building*
- *Peak Performance*

To learn more about Aaron Davis Presentations please visit www.aarondavisspeaks.com. You may also call us toll-free at 1.800.474.8755 or send an email to: adavis@aarondavisspeaks.com.

Introduction

Today matters because it's all that you and I have. There is absolutely nothing we can do about yesterday, but there is plenty that we can do about today. Tomorrow is not guaranteed, so why rob today of it's opportunities? The only thing that you and I can control in our lives is what we do with the time we have today. This book was written to remind you of what really matters and what you can do each day to get the most out of your life.

Though I grew up the youngest of six kids in a home that didn't have much money, my parents taught us the true meaning of success and happiness. Many of those lessons can be found within the pages of this book. Over the past ten years I've spent hundreds of hours reading thousands of articles and books in my quest to unearth characteristics of people who make the most of each day. To my surprise, much of the information I learned was almost identical to the simple but powerful truths that my loving mother and father instilled in me and my other siblings.

Today, the average life span is around 25,550 days. Why not take just fifty of those days and allow this book to remind you that they all count and that the older we get, the faster they go. My hope is for you to grow spiritually & mentally as a result of these 10 Minute Truths. Happy Reading!

Your Days Are Limited

We all get 86,400 seconds everyday.
The tragedy is that most people just let it slip by.
-Aaron Davis

Today is your day, because you are going to do things today that you have never done before! Do you know why? Today is brand new. Yesterday ended last night, and you have been given a fresh twenty-four hours.

"Time is the coin of your life. It is the only coin you have, and only you can determine how it will be spent. Be careful lest you let other people spend it for you". ~Carl Sandberg

What you do with today is totally in your hands. When you live to seize each day, it doesn't matter what side of the bed you wake up on. Either side is going to be just fine for the person who is determined to make each day count.

1. **Today, seize the day, your day, by just smiling at as many people as you possibly can, just to see how it feels.** How in the world can smiling make one feel better? The next time you get angry or frustrated with yourself or with someone else, try smiling and see if you can continue to be as angry. According to an article featured Dentalplans.com, smiling has proven to lower heart rate and produce less stressful and rapid breathing. It also stated that when we do smile, it makes us happier. With all of these known benefits of smiling, how can you not at least "try" it and see if it doesn't make a tremendous impact in your life, both personally and professionally?

2. **Do one "fun" thing today that you have been putting off.** Some people feel that if they take some time from their day to do something "fun," they are wasting time. This simply is not

true. In fact, doing something fun energizes you and helps you relax. Doing something fun gives you pleasure and refreshes you at the same time. Work hard of course, don't forget to play hard as well!

3. **What is one small thing that you could do today that would improve your life?** Think about this for a moment. Each of us know several things we could do to dramatically improve our lives. Simply getting up earlier would help you avoid the stress and anxiety associated with rushing to make it to work on time. Have that dreaded conversation with that important person in your life that you've been avoiding. Actually go to that gym that you pay sixty dollars a month to belong to! The beauty of doing just one small thing is that you'll reap big rewards by accomplishing it. If you want to start reaping big rewards in your life on a daily basis, then start doing the small things first!

2

Selfishness is Counterproductive

No duty is more urgent than that of returning thanks.
-St. Ambrose

Share the Wealth

I was fortunate enough to have played college football for one of the greatest coaches of all time, Dr. Tom Osborne. As the head football coach at the University of Nebraska-Lincoln for over twenty-five years, he won three National Championships. When it was all said and done, Coach Osborne walked away from college football as one of the Winningests coaches of all time. Some have referred to him as a genius when it came to picking apart the opposing team's defensive schemes and strategies. Although everyone knew he was brilliant, you would never hear him say anything remotely arrogant. Instead of taking all the glory and accolades for himself, he would always divert the attention to the players, assistant coaches, administration, and all the other crucial, yet often under appreciated, individuals who make up a winning team.

My speaking and consulting business would be nowhere near where it is today if not for the wisdom and knowledge of other people I work closely with. One person in particular is my business strategist, Todd Kelley. Todd is one of my best friends and one of the smartest people I know. Having successful stints with major corporations and being a successful business owner himself, he has knowledge that I don't have and understands certain things that I just don't understand. I realize that Todd is a tremendous asset to my future success and I constantly remind him of my sincere appreciation for him.

Whether your company boasts over 100,000 worldwide clients or you are the owner of a small three-person specialty store, share the wealth when praise and prestige come your way. No one can do it alone.

I don't believe in SELF-MADE people. In my opinion, there are only HELP-MADE people. Share the wealth. It lasts longer that way.

Call, write or email just one person today who has helped you in the past, and just say thank you!

Deciding Who You Are Is Key

I don't want to get to the end of my life and find that I have just lived the length of it. I want to have lived the width of it as well.
-Diane Ackerman

Define Your Line

I'm the type of person who likes to look at the obituary section in my morning paper while I drink my coffee. Weird, huh? Let me explain why. You see, I like to look at who and what people have left behind. I'm always curious about their accomplishments, what their children's names were, how many grandchildren they had, how they made their living, etc. I'm always probing to find out what type of legacy people leave behind to their loved ones. Though reading the obituary section doesn't tell you very much about their personality or love for their friends and family, it does provide some evidence they have actually walked this earth.

When I think about all the great individuals who have shaped our world, those known and unknown, they've all left huge prints on this earth. Think about Harriet Tubman and the Underground Railroad that freed thousands of slaves from the horrible grip of slavery. How about Russell Conwell whose famous book, *Acres of Diamonds,* has touched millions of lives over the years. There is the great track star, Wilma Rudolph; the ever compassionate and giving Mother Theresa; and millions more who have shaped our world by knowing exactly who they were. They gave and impacted each of us in some way or another.

What is going to render evidence that you actually walked the earth? Think about it for a moment. Sure, you probably have a job, friends and family, but that's not what I'm referring to. I'm talking about the legacy that you're going to leave behind. Every day, each of us is defining our line. The line that I'm referring to will be the one that rests on every tombstone. The line that separates the words Born and Died. Only you can define what that line will or will not stand for. Only you can determine the relationships you form; only you can pour yourself into your goals and dreams; only you can choose to forgive; only you can decide to speak a word of encouragement; only you can put every ounce of energy towards the gifts and talents that God has bestowed upon you. The line isn't very exotic and it doesn't have any special qualities to it - it's simple and straightforward. It's up to you to define the line, my friend.

1. What type of legacy do you want to leave behind?

2. How would you want your friends, family, and co-workers to describe you if they were to speak at your funeral?

3.If you're not the type of person you want to be remembered as, what can you do to begin changing that?

Opportunity Knocks-Can you Answer?

*The reason so many people never get anywhere in life is
because when opportunities knock, they are out in the
backyard looking for four-leaf clovers.*
–Walter P. Chrysler

Position Yourself for Opportunities

There was a man who loved to take his family to the town parade that
was held each summer. The parade was the event of the summer for
the whole town and the surrounding area. The town called Missed Opportunity was made up of only 500 people, but on parade day it would
double and sometimes triple in size. The man and his family always had
a wonderful time looking at all the floats and listening to the marching
bands as they blasted their instruments and walked in unison down the
street. The only problem was that each year, the man and his family
could never seem to get there early enough to find a good place from
which to watch the parade. The man was constantly lifting up each one
of his three children so they could see the parade as it went by.

As the summer parade was drawing near again, the man said to himself, "This year, I will camp out the night before the parade, on the edge
of the street, right where the parade will pass by. Then, my family and I
shall surely have a good place to view the day's events."

So the man and his family camped out the night before, positioning
themselves right one the edge of the street where last year's parade had
taken place. The excitement over the over the next day's events kept the
man's family up most of the night. They talked about how wonderful it
would be to finally see the colorful floats and clowns and hear, up close,
the blare of the instruments as the bands passed by.

The waiting was almost unbearable for them all, but finally it was
morning and as the sun began to peek over the morning clouds. The
town began to stir with excitement and anticipation. However, something
seemed strange. As the parade time drew near, the man noticed that no
one was coming to the street to set up chairs or bleachers. He didn't see
the cotton candy machine swirling around with bright pink candy wait-

ing to melt in the children's mouths. He didn't smell the fresh scent of popcorn dripping with butter. There were no people milling around. He didn't hear a single trombone or flute warming up for the march through the streets. In fact, he didn't see anybody with a two-block radius. When the start of the parade was only a few minutes away, he began to see people walking by him and his family, heading three blocks down the street. After seeing several dozen people walk by, he finally asked some-one where they were going. They responded that they were on their way to the parade down the street, to which the man replied, "I thought that the parade was starting here." The people informed him that the parade route had been changed and that the change had been announced on the previous night's radio news. At that moment, the man realized that he had camped out in the wrong street.

Like this man, many of us have positioned ourselves in what we thought were great places to seize opportunities, only to find that we had positioned ourselves in the wrong place. Many people wonder why opportunities always seem to be on the others side of the street (or within another company), when the truth is, the opportunities they so desperately seek would be within their grasp if they only positioned themselves in the correct place. Too many people are missing parades of opportunity because they have failed to educate themselves on the details of the very thing they seek to have. When you begin to properly position yourself, you will become the beneficiary of numerous opportunities. There are three ways that you can start to position yourself for opportunities:

1. **Know What it is You Want** -- If you don't know what you want, it's not likely that you'll get anything. Take time to stop and think about what you desire spiritually, emotionally, physically, and socially.

2. **Decide to Pay the Price** -- It's not enough just to know what you want. You have to be willing to pay the price. In order to get what you want, you have to be willing to resist temporary gratification.

3. **Keep Striving** -- After you begin to seize opportunities and ben-efit from them, don't stop there. Refuse to become complacent with your accomplishments and success. Continue to challenge yourself, to climb higher mountains and explore deeper waters.

Failure is an Integral Part of Life

*Our greatest glory is not in ever falling, but
in rising every time we fall.*
-Confucius

Give Yourself Freedom to Fail

Where does failure live? Does it have an address? When was it born? Who are the parents of failure? All of the above questions are absurd! Like the inspirational speaker and author Zig Ziglar states, "Failure is only an event." Nothing else. If it becomes anything more than that, it's only because you have decided to make it more. You see, friend, there is not a single person alive who has not experienced the painful event of failure.

When I was in college, I took a business statistics class that was so difficult for me, I would have nightmares about it. I found myself waking up in the middle of the night because I was having a terrible dream about some of the formulas and theories that I needed to know for exams and projects. I had never studied so hard for a class only to fail miserably on every exam, except one. (That's right, I only passed one exam the entire course, and on the one that I did pass, I think the professor passed me only because he felt sorry for me).

When my semester grades arrived in the mail, I immediately looked for my statistics grade and there it was---a giant D. That's right, a D. My attendance and daily assignments landed me the passing grade. If you'd seen my reaction upon discovering this, you would have thought I just made the dean's list. I was jumping up and down, racing around my house. You may be wondering how anyone could be so ecstatic about a D, one grade above failing. In many people's eyes, this would have been a failure. But not in my eyes, because God knows I gave that class every ounce of energy and focus that I could muster. When you put all you've got into something, what more can you give? Failure is inevitable in one's quest for success. I may have received a D for that statistics class, but the education that I received about myself was priceless. I've learned that failure serves as a strong foundation for success when you

8

take the opportunity to learn from it.

Failure Simply Tells You What Won't Work

Have you ever tried to open your car door with very little light and your hands are somewhat full? You try one key after another until you find the correct one. You open the door, put in your things and you're on your way. Most people wouldn't stop trying only after one or two failures from their keys. They would keep trying because with each "failure" they know that they are getting closer to their desired outcome. In other words failure is simply finding out which key doesn't work.

Others Will Remind You

Anytime you attempt "BIG" things in life, you have to be prepared to deal with people. You see, people are often the main reasons that many individuals quit after receiving feedback from failure. These people hardly ever fail because they rarely attempt anything "BIG" so to avoid failure. The thing that you have to remember is that if you're failing, at least you're doing something, unlike those pitiful souls that attempt nothing at all!

Look for Answers

A fantastic way to deal with failure (feedback) is to seek answers from the situation. You can always find answers if you look hard enough. As a former athlete, I always looked the hardest after a loss because you can learn more in a loss than you can in a win, but you must not be afraid of what you'll find. Be diligent and aggressive in finding answers during failure.

Self-talk Can Be Dangerous

A person's self-talk has a way of manifesting those things talked about most. If another person called you the names you call yourself, how would you feel?
-Aaron Davis

Watch Your Mind's Mouth

- How could I be so stupid?
- Everybody is so much smarter than me.
- I'm too old.
- I'm too young.
- I don't have enough experience.
- I'll never be able to lose weight.
- My parents will never be proud of me.
- I just can't be a good husband or wife.
- I just don't have it in me to be a good mother or father.
- I'm never going to get that promotion.

Remember the old saying, "Sticks and stones may break my bones, but words will never hurt me?" This is an ABSOLUTE LIE! Words do hurt. Unfortunately, we are hurting ourselves more than anyone else with the inner dialogue, or self-talk, that each of us engages in on a daily basis. What words do you use when you talk about yourself? There is power in inner dialogue. Have you ever gotten up in the morning to the blare of your alarm and said to yourself, "Just another day at the job I hate?" Your feet haven't even hit the floor and your day is already off to a bad start because of the message that you just gave your sub-conscious. If you tell yourself something often enough, your brain eventually believes it. Changing the way you talk to yourself can be the first step in changing your life.

Words Have Power!
For as he thinketh in his heart, so is he.
Proverbs 23:7

My friend you are exactly where you are in life because of the words you use, internally and externally. Words have the power to create both the beauty and the ugly in your life; it totally depends on you. Your internal dialogue has the awesome ability to create all sorts of emotions. Emotions create Actions. Actions create results. If you don't like the results that your words have been creating, then it's time to change your words.

Without proper discipline and diligence you can't change your internal dialogue to render the results that you desire. In order to think well, you must flood your mind with thoughts and talk of growth, faith and hope. Obviously just thinking about it will not change your life. You must take action! All the positive thinking in the world cannot replace action. It's imperative that you put feet on your thoughts!

Here are three things you can do to improve your inner dialogue:

1. **Become more aware of your inner dialogue**. For just one day, write down the number of negative comments that you make towards yourself. This exercise alone can assist you in becoming more aware of how condescending you can be towards yourself.

2. **Replace your negative comments with positive ones**. For example, instead of saying, "This is going to be a horrible day," rephrase this by saying, "I have been blessed to awake another day." Instead of saying, "I'm never going to get that promotion," you could say, "I'm going to take the necessary steps to improve myself and my performance so that I give myself a greater chance at receiving that promotion."

3. **Do what Myles Davis taught me**. No, not the famous deceased jazz musician, Miles Davis, but my dad, Myles Davis. Growing up, he always taught our family to pat ourselves on the back, in the knowledge that we were champions. People don't give themselves enough credit for the talents and abilities that they have within them. God made you a champion, start talking like one!

People Are Our Most Important Resources

*All of us, at certain moments in our lives, need to
take advice and to receive help from other people.*
–Alexis Carrel

Value People

It's been said that some companies and organizations spend close to 80% of their money on their employees' incomes, but less than 2% on showing them how much they actually value their contributions and talents.

This unfortunate reality is pervasive not only in the business arena but in day-to-day interactions as well: the husband who neglects his wife while trying to climb the corporate ladder, leaving a trail of broken promises and tattered relationships behind him; the working woman who put so much time and effort into breaking through the glass ceiling that they forgot whose shoulders they stood on in order to reach their destination. Some college students think success is getting all A's. Meanwhile, focusing on getting A's might lead them to miss out on the college experience because they isolate themselves for four years.

We Need People

Not a single success story exists about a person who achieved great things without the help and support of someone else. Not a single one! Each of us must rely on the resources, intelligence, gifts, and talents of others if we want to accomplish anything in life. Even simple day-to-day chores could not be accomplished without the direct or indirect help from other people. Think about this the next time you find yourself in an airplane. Pilots receive all the envy and adoration. Don't get me wrong. Anyone who can takeoff and land a huge aircraft going over 400 miles per hour at times deserves a great deal of credit but let's look a little deeper. Each time that plane lands it's refueled, checked over, cleaned out and made airworthy by dozens of other people. The plane would have a hard time even knowing where to park and take off from if it wasn't for the people in the control tower. **ALL PEOPLE NEED PEOPLE!**

Look at things from their Porch

Remember the first time you went over to your neighbor's house and stood on the porch and glanced across the street at your place and saw how different it looked? If you look at things from your own front porch you can only see things from your perspective. In order to really appreciate people and their contributions and perspectives, you have to get off your own porch sometimes and see what they see! Try to experience what they are experiencing. I'm not saying that you have to compromise who you are and what you stand for, but you do have to understand that everyone is not always going to see things from your point of view.

Tell People Thank You & Be Specific

It's amazing how many people fail to say thank you to those who directly help them succeed. I'm so used to some cashiers not saying thank-you that I make it a point to stand there and say "thank you," and then wait for a response. The sad thing is, some look at me in bewilderment and even ask if I need anything else; To one cashier I responded, "Yes, I would like for you to tell me thank you for purchasing my goods here so that you can have a paycheck"…still no response; only a clueless look on their face.

I'm very adamant about specific praise and appreciation for the big and small things in my daily life. Gratitude, even for the smallest acts, renders big results and almost ensures that the service will be handled in the same manner next time. If you want your family, your company, your friends or even your local grocer to render better service, sometimes just letting them know that you appreciate them for what they do for you is all it takes. Be specific. Let them know what you are thankful for and explain to them how that makes things easier for you. I guarantee you'll get a few weird looks at first because it's so rare when it actually happens.

In our efforts to attain success, it's all to easy to neglect the ones we love and trust the most. People should be and must be held in high-esteem, no matter what title comes before their name or how many letters come after it. It's not enough to say that you value relationships and support of those around you. You have to SHOW IT!

1. When was the last time you "showed" your family how much you appreciate them?

2. Do the people you work with and work for "know" that you value them? How?

Your Environment Determines Your Destiny

*We begin to see, therefore, the importance of selecting
our environments with the greatest of care, because
environment is the mental feeding ground out of which
the food that goes into our minds is extracted.*
–Napoleon Hill

Create an Environment Conducive to Success

Many people have all the right tools for success. They know exactly
what they want. They have a well thought-out plan to achieve their objectives and they have a burning desire as fuel for the journey. But even
with all of these areas accounted for, millions still come up short when
trying to reach their full potential because they have overlooked one important thing that plays a pivotal role in success: their environment. You
must consciously create an environment that brings out the best in you.

Check Your Surroundings Regularly

It's tough to succeed in life when your own environment poses greater
obstacles than those found in the real world. I'm not talking about the
factors that you can't control, such as your parents, or the way your feet
look in sandals. I'm talking about the place that you call your office
or where you do your thinking, planning, and working. This may be
your home office or the sixty-eighth floor, high above the streets. The
geographical location is secondary. The most important thing to consider is whether or not it's helping you reach your maximum potential.
You must be proactive in checking your surroundings on a regular basis. The damage sustained from negative environments doesn't happen
overnight. It's a gradual process that, if left unchecked, can set you back
years in your progress.

Championship Environment

When I played football for the University of Nebraska in the early nineties, we were head and shoulders about the rest of the college football
teams when it came to strength and conditioning. At that time Nebraska

boasted a 30,000 square foot weight room, one of the largest weight rooms in the world during that time. Talk about a great environment to get the body in shape! I can say from experience that just by walking into that weight room you felt like grabbing a dumbbell and curling a few sets or perhaps getting under the squat rack and squatting a few sets.

Besides a world class weight room, the University of Nebraska also featured a brand-new luxury skybox section for fans and corporate sponsors to enjoy while watching their team compete. Last, but definitely not least, the university has one of the top student athlete graduation rates in the entire nation. The academic support and the facilities ranked second to none. Of course, I'm biased as an alumnus of UNL, but facts are facts. The University of Nebraska has made it a priority to create a Championship environment for its student athletes to be successful on and off the field. It's no wonder during the nineties the Nebraska football team claimed three National Championships (1994,1995,1997) while continuing to serve as a leader in Academic All-Americans as well!

Make It Work For You

Anyone who is serious about success must create an environment that assists rather than hinder them in reaching their full potential. If you want to be successful, you must surround yourself with successful people and resources. You must create an atmosphere that gives you the best chance at obtaining your goals. Perhaps you need to build up your personal library of books, or maybe you need to organize your desk and the mounting unread email messages in your in box. It could be a number of things. The key is to make your environment into one that helps, rather than hinders your progress.

On a scale of 1-5 with one meaning "excellent" and five meaning "very poor," how would you rate your personal environment (people you surround yourself with, social network, etc.)? How would you rate your professional environment (your work space, relationships, contacts, etc.)? If you're not satisfied with your rating, guess what? You can change them. So get started immediately at making your environment conducive to success!

Life is Going to Shake You Up

Do not be quickly provoked in your spirit,
for anger resides in the lap of fools.
-Ecclesiastes 7:9

If you've ever dropped a can of soda and then were daring enough to open it up right away you know exactly what happens. You twist open the top and because the carbon contained within that can was shaken up, it shoots all over the place! As humans, we are not much different than that shaken can of soda. Life is full of incidents that shake us up. It's a tragedy that so many of us forget that we have the power to decide how we will respond once shaken up. Remember the "hockey dad" incident that took place on July 5, 2001? Thomas Junta beat to death another man after a youth hockey practice in which both men's son's participated. That single act of rage, which lasted only moments, resulted in a life of pain for both families involved. Thomas Junta had an experience that shook him up and, unfortunately, he failed to control his anger. As a result, two families are now forced to go on without fathers and husbands.

Anger shows what's inside
People tend to show who and what they really are when life shakes them up. If you ever want to know what lies deep within a person, watch how they respond to life when it shakes them up. Jobs have been lost, marriages destroyed, and relationships damaged beyond repair as a result of an individual unable to properly vent their anger.

Vent Baby Vent!
Everybody gets angry. In fact, we need more people to get angry with some of the conditions that we face in our world today! I'm not referring to righteous indignation. No, I'm referring to the self-destructing type of anger that, if not properly kept in check, can cause a lot of damage within seconds. How do you avoid this? Vent, Baby, Vent!

Find ways that you can vent and release your anger and frustration. Go running, walking, or play sports. Hit the weights instead of the wall! Do anything, just make sure that you get the anger out of your system in a way that's not going to physically hurt yourself or others. Sometimes simply stepping away from the situation for a few minutes, hours or even days can work wonders and help resolve the issue.

Don't be Naïve

One of the biggest mistakes that we often make is failing to recognize our own capacity to do some "dumb" things when we are angry. When you know what your anger is capable of and take proactive steps in order to keep it in check, you could truly be saving your own life and the life of others.

It's an Episode

An angry phone call, attacking emails, cars that cut you off in traffic are all simply examples of episodes. They are not a life sentence unless you make them such. I'm not saying that anger is supposed to make you feel great, but keep in mind that the current situation will not be so current next week or next year unless you keep giving it life.

Forgive Me

Truly successful people ask for forgiveness if they have offended anyone as a result of their anger going unchecked. It always takes a bigger person to say, "I'm sorry." It's the little people who fight tooth and nail to avoid apologizing.

Life is going to shake you up from time to time. The question is, how will you respond?

1. Do you like the way that you respond when life shakes you up?

2. You have the power to decide how to respond to a situation when you get angry. Do you have a "strategy" in place so that when you get angry you can vent properly? If not, take a few moments to devise one. It's always better to prepare than to repair.

3. Think of a time that your anger got the best of you and the damage it caused. What could you have done differently?

Wishing Alone Gets You Nowhere

Understand that most problems are a good sign. Problems indicate that progress is being made, wheels are turning and you are moving towards your goal. Beware when you have no problems. Then you've really got a problem. Problems are landmarks of progress.
–Scott Alexander

Stop Wishing the Problem Will Go Away and Deal with It
I wish I had a better job. I wish I had a better relationship with my children. I wish I had a bigger home. I wish, I wish, I wish….

Ever had a bad case of the "I wishes?" We've all uttered this phrase at one time or another in our lives. The problem with the "I wishes" is that wishing never gets you any closer to solving your problems. The only way to solve a problem is to decide to solve it. That's it. No magic solution, no thunders across the sky, no big "Eureka!" experience -- you just have to do it.

People often destroy any chance of advancing toward the things they really want in life because they refuse to stop wishing that their problems didn't exist. The very moment that you decide that you have had enough of wishing and want to start doing, your life will change immediately.

Disgust is the Answer
You can deal with the problems in your life by first becoming disgusted with your current situation. Disgust is a strong emotion and it's a powerful agent for change. You must become so disgusted with your lack of action that you can do nothing but look the problem in the face and stand up to it. Secondly, you must fight the temptation to retreat to familiar territory. Any time we are faced with an uncomfortable situation, we almost immediately seek the people and things that are familiar to us, even if those people and things are the very things we are trying to eliminate from our lives. A perfect example of this is the high recidivism rate of inmates who, once released, end up right back in jail. Why does

this happen? Well, there are several reasons, but the most notable is an inability to refrain from going back to the life of crime that was harmful (but familiar) to them in the first place. The same holds true for the large number of people in domestic violence situations. Familiarity can be fatal. Life is too short and too precious to continue wishing for change. If you want to solve the problems in your life, you need to do but one thing -- decide!

1. What situation in your life right now causes you the most frustration? Are you really disgusted with it or just tired of it? Remember you must be disgusted before you can really embark on any long lasting change.

2. Take just ten minutes and decide to do one thing about that area of your life that is causing you the most disgust. A word of caution here: your heart must be involved. It's from our hearts that REAL change takes place.

The Past Can Ruin The Future

Death is not the greatest loss in life.
The greatest loss is what dies inside us while we live.
-Norman Cousins

Let Go

The only way you can take hold of each day with enthusiasm is to let go of yesterday's pain and defeats. Too many people allow yesterday to destroy their today and darken their tomorrow. Sure, life can be tough, and even downright unfair, but it's up to you to decide how you're going to respond to the frequent storms of life.

June 24, 1996, is a day that will live with me forever. This was the day my roommate and close friend since childhood was murdered. Those of you reading who've lost a loved one can relate to the feeling of loss and the incredible pain I was feeling inside. Although it's been 12 years since my friend died, I miss him terribly.

Life is full of pain. How we deal with the pain makes all the difference in the world. After his death, I remember one day in particular that I was having a really hard time. I began to think about all the good times we'd shared over the years. As I looked at my watch, I realized that I had zoned out for over an hour, thinking about all the memories with my friend. That day, I decided to let go. Not of the memories and good times that we'd shared, but of the anger and hatred growing in my heart towards the individual responsible for his death.

How to Let Go
To err is human; to forgive, Divine
-Alexander Pope

You forgive ***one day at a time***. Each day you must make a ***conscious decision*** to either control your emotions or allow the painful emotions to control you. You are not forgiving for the other person(s)' sake; you are forgiving for your own peace of mind.

When you harbor unforgiveness in your heart, you allow that painful situation to be the final story. By forgiving, you're rewriting the script! It doesn't mean that you forget the pain, but rather you allow the pain to help you grow and mature. ***Pain never enters one's life without leaving a learning experience behind***. Instead of focusing only on the pain, you have to make a "choice" to search for the lesson and message as well.

God has given mankind free will or choice. Choice is always present when dealing with forgiveness. You have the choice to forgive or not but you WILL face the consequences of choosing to hang onto your pain; that's why it's imperative to let go if you want to experience peace of mind.

Sometimes, life requires us to let go of one thing in order to hold on tighter to something else that is of greater value. Maybe you have something that you're holding on to that you've been meaning to let go of. The only thing holding you back is you.

1. What is holding you back from letting go of the hurt, anger, and pain that you may have suffered in the past?

2. Pray and ask God to help you heal, one day at a time.

It's the Little Things That Get You

*Never measure the significance of anything by
its size or lack thereof.*
-Aaron Davis

Avoid the Titanic Incident

One of the worst disasters in maritime history took place just before midnight on April 14, 1912. Of the more than 2,200 persons aboard the Titanic, 1,513 died. The ship had been proclaimed to be virtually unsinkable prior to that dreadful evening. Originally, many thought that only a huge tear in the ship's hull could have caused the massive ship to sink. However, in the wake of the disaster, a naval architect named Edward Wilding testified that the total area damaged by the iceberg was small and probably didn't exceed one square meter (about twelve square feet). Others didn't believe that such a small tear could have caused this ship to sink.

Later, sonar findings confirmed Wilding's belief that the damage had been slight. There were six thin breaches spread out along a 35 m (110ft) section of the hull, with a total surface area of about 1 sq. m.

You may be wondering what any of this has to do with you and your journey to success. Think about it for a moment. When you suffer major disappointments or setbacks in your personal and professional life, you generally tend to look at the massive gashes or the big icebergs you might have run into.

Many times, it's not the major gashes that have caused our hopes, dreams, and relationships to sink. Often, it's the small breaches in our lives that eventually lead us to sink into our own personal abyss. The small things that we neglect usually end up causing us the most pain later.

Ask yourself these questions:

1. What are three "small" things that I could do today that could have a major impact on my personal and professional life?

2. What would my life look like if I did these three things?

3. How would I feel if I did these three things? Less stress, anger, peace, joy?

4. What are the consequences if I continue to ignore these three small things?

Ask yourself these questions often and follow up on the answers to avoid a Titanic incident in your life.

13

We Have Two Ears and One Mouth for a Reason

The jungle speaks to me because I know how to listen.
-Mowgli from The Jungle Book

Take the Time to Listen

The first time that I visited my wife's family pig farm, I had a life changing experience. It was during our college dating years, and I went home with her for a weekend to really get a feel for the hog-farming industry. I was in for a rude awakening! From our conversations, Brooke (my wife) never really told me how many pigs they had. I just figured maybe a few dozen or so. WRONG!!

This hog farm is located in central Nebraska in the middle of nowhere, but the surrounding area is absolutely beautiful (with the exception of the smell of course, but you get used to that, since they claim it smells like money).

While I was riding along with my future father-in-law, Jeff, in his truck, he gave me the tour of this major operation. It turned out that thousands of hogs went through this farm each year! I was in utter amazement at the number of pigs I was seeing and the technology involved in the computerized automation used in the feeding systems. Here I was, this farming illiterate, totally blown away by the sophistication of this major operation.

As I took the tour, Jeff introduced me to a task that to this day, still gives me goose bumps. There are literally dozens of jobs that have to be done on a farm each day, or the consequences become very costly. One of those jobs is "power washing". To those of you who have no idea what power washing is, hang on -- I'm about to explain it to you.

To those of you who know exactly what I'm talking about, please cease from laughing and continue reading, because you haven't read anything yet. To perform this task, you need to be wearing the right gear, which includes a set of long boots, rain gear, and goggles (but don't plan on ever wearing any of these articles of clothing again, except on a farm). After putting on the proper attire for this mystery task, Jeff led me into one of several pig units, where some of the pigs were housed. As we were walking to the hog building, the smell began to quickly intensify, but it was nothing compared to what I was in for. Once in the hog building, I couldn't believe me eyes (or my nose for that matter). There were pigs all over the building in penned sections, and it seemed like the moment I walked through the door, all of their eyes were on me.

First, he told me to remove all the pigs from the caged sections and to herd them into the hallway. I thought to myself, "Hey, no problem, I'll just open the cages and the pigs will walk toward the other end of the building in a nice single file line so I can section them off and let the cleaning take place."

Boy, was I wrong! Trying to herd pigs is like trying to herd water. Those smelly suckers were running all over the place and I think Jeff got a real kick out of watching these hogs make a fool out of me as I was slipping and sliding in you-know-what.

After finally getting all of the pigs to the other end of the building, I was taught the craft of power washing. Power washing is simply spraying hot water (about 130-140 degrees) out of a long hose to clean the pens where the pigs have been (and you know what pigs tend to leave behind). Well, this was my job for the next few hours. As Jeff was explaining some last-minute details to me, I was already getting started. Because I was only hearing what he was saying and not really "listening," I learned a lifelong lesson. I was moving right along during the washing process and even beginning to think this whole thing was somewhat therapeutic, because it gave me time to think even with the repugnant smell. In fact, I became so relaxed while spraying that I even began to whistle and then sing. BIG, BIG MISTAKE!

As I was singing and spraying, all of a sudden, gulp! Something (you know what) had somehow made it's way into my mouth for a direct hit! It happened so fast that I didn't have much time to process what just happened until the roof of my mouth and stomach begin sending signals to my brain that something was terribly wrong. I begin to quickly feel dizzy and a little nauseous. I turned off the sprayer and leaned against the wall to collect myself and I begin to think back to when Jeff was giving me the instructions and explaining the details that, in my haste, I failed to listen to. One of the most important rules of power washing is "Never, never power wash with your mouth open!"

Hearing will Cost You . . . and You will Pay!

When you choose to only "hear" others instead of listening to them it will cost you. It will cost you personally, professionally and in almost every other area in your life. We often hear -- the following phrase, "You just aren't listening to me!"

Maybe the key relationships in your life have been severed or seriously strained as a result of only thinking of what you're going to say next instead of listening to them share what's really on their heart. The best way to alienate close friends or the loved ones in your life is to simply not listen to them. Listening is one of the most simple things that we can do to strengthen and grow our relationships, but it's not always easy.

When God created us, he gave us two ears and one mouth. I think that's a clue that we should listen twice as much as we talk.

Honor The Person Speaking

Think about a time when you met someone who was very distinguished or famous. Your eyes followed them with every move they made no matter if they were singing, dancing, speaking or just simply standing there looking around. You showed complete reverence and honor towards this person. The word *honor* is defined as "admiring or giving tribute to someone or something" and that's exactly what we can show to others by simply "listening" to them.

Don't listen at All!

If you're too busy to give a person your undivided attention don't listen to them at all! Politely let them know that now is not a good time but then give them a specific time that would be better and that you'll be all ears. Or kindly tell them that you have five minutes and that if it will take longer you will be happy to schedule an appointment with them. This type of courtesy is seldom ill received. Try it!

14
Fear and Faith Cannot Co-Exist

"Fear and Faith are like oil and water. They don't mix."
-Aaron Davis

Choose Faith over Fear

The Bible says that faith can move mountains. Studies over the years continue to show that patients with faith who have been diagnosed with various illnesses tend to recover more quickly than those who don't demonstrate a deep faith and belief that they eventually will overcome their illness.

So what is faith? A great example of faith verse fear or belief can be found in this story . . .

There was a great tightrope walker known as the Great Blondin. In the late 1890's he strung a tightrope across Niagra Falls, and then before thousands of screaming people, he made his way from the Canadian side of the falls to the U.S. side. When he got there, the crowd was in sheer pandemonium shouting his name, "Blondin! Blondin! Blondin!"

Finally he raised his arms to quite the crowd and he shouted this to them, "I am Blondin! Do you believe in me?" The crowd shouted back, "We believe! We believe! We believe!" Again he quieted the crowd and once more he shouted to them, "I'm going back across the tightrope but this time I'm going to carry someone on my back. Do you believe I can do that?" The crowd yelled, "We believe! We believe!" He quieted them one more time and then he said, "Who will be that person?" The crowd went dead. Nothing. Finally out of the crowd stepped one man. He climbed on Blondin's shoulders and for the next three and a half hours, Blondin inched his way back across the tightrope to the Canadian side of the falls.

The whole crowd said that they believed when no "action" had to be taken in order to validate their belief or faith. Only one man truly believed and had faith in Blondin. True faith and belief move you to take "action". Where would you fit in this illustration?

When you truly believe in something, there is very little that can thwart your efforts. Several things happen once you exercise your faith.

Unwavering Faith Allows You to Live with Passion

When I get a chance, I like to watch those "Extreme" sports shows on ESPN when I'm channel surfing. You see people on skateboards, bikes, and roller blades doing things that seem impossible. I have seen ramps reaching heights of over twenty feet tall being jumped over with amazing precision and skill. Guys on roller blades zoom down a sidewalk at break-neck speeds and in one harmonious motion, they launch themselves into the air and land skillfully along a ledge that's only about three foot wide. Some of you may think this has nothing to do with faith but sheer craziness. I beg to differ. I think its faith in action, which equals sheer PASSION!

Here is my little formula: $F + A = P$ (Faith + Action = Passion).

Faith Provides Energy & Confidence to Overcome Obstacles

When I was in sixth grade my mother suffered a major stroke at the young age of 42. She did not drink or smoke and was in relatively good health. Upon hearing the news regarding my mother, I remember being devastated because of severity of the stroke. My mother wasn't able to speak very well and couldn't walk. The first time that I saw her in the hospital seemed surreal. You see, my mother is a very strong woman, both mentally and physically. To see her in a condition in which she couldn't care for herself was hard. She couldn't talk clearly or walk on her own and the situation looked very grim in regards to her making a full recovery. But faith has a way of overcoming the obstacles.

While my mother lay in her hospital bed she began to exercise the power of faith by telling all who would listen that she was going to beat this stroke. In fact when visitors would come to the hospital to see my mother, she would speak to them and encourage them. After visiting with my mother you knew that her present "condition" was only temporary and not life-long because of the amazing "faith" that she displayed even though she was facing a long uphill climb with many obstacles in the way.

To the amazement of her doctors and physical therapists, my mother began to literally talk to her legs and hands. She would tell her hands to move and her legs to step. My mother is the epitome of how a strong faith mixed with passion can render amazing results no matter what obstacles lay ahead.

It is not death that a man should fear, but he
should fear never beginning to live.
Marcus Aurelius –Roman Emperor 121-80 A.D.

Turn on the lights!

Growing up, my brother and I had bunk beds; I slept on the bottom bunk. Those bunk beds provided us with all sorts of fun from hanging blankets down the sides and making it into our own submarine, to using the top bunk as diving board and jumping into a pile of pillows down below. Those bunk beds provided me with all sorts of fun and adventure. But when the lights were turned out, those very same bunk beds became the source of terror at night.

The four posts that held up our bunk beds also served as places to hang our coats or robes at night. When the lights went out, those coats and robes with their oversized forms, looked like oversized figures standing there, looking at you. The more I allowed irrational thoughts to enter my mind, the bigger and more terrorizing those coats became. Finally after spending most of one night in absolute fear I slowly got out of bed and ran towards the lights, switched them on, and saw those oversized shadows for what they really were -- NOTHING!!

Many times we allow oversized shadows of nothing to dominate our thoughts, robbing us of truly living a life of purpose and passion!

The best way to deal with fear is to meet it head on. You may have heard that fear is the acronym for False Evidence Appearing Real and that's exactly what it is.

"One of the greatest discoveries a man makes, one of his great surprises, is to find he can do what he was afraid he couldn't do."
-Henry Ford

Moments Make Up Our Lives

Right now, a moment of time is passing by.
We must become that moment.
-Paul Cezanne

Capture the Moments

I had just returned from a three-day business trip and my wife, Brooke, and my oldest son, Aden (who was two at the time), were waiting for me in the airport. This was pre 9/11, when your family or friends could wait for you right where the passengers exited the plane. As soon as Aden's little eyes met mine, he began to run as fast as he could towards me with his little red cheeks and a big smile painted across his face. He got to me yelling "Daddy, Daddy," and as I reached down to pick him up, my cell phone rang.

There it was, I hadn't seen my son in over three days, and instead of ignoring the phone and letting the voicemail do what it's supposed to do, I answered the call. Instead of concentrating on my little guy, who wanted to see his Daddy, I focused on the caller. I missed that moment.

Moments that Moved the World

On December 1, 1955 Rosa Parks unknowingly seized her moment in time when she became the "mother" of the civil rights movement. After a long day at work as a seamstress in downtown Montgomery, Alabama, Rosa Parks boarded the bus and sat down to rest. After refusing to get up out of her seat to make way for one of the white passengers she incited a national movement that would forever change the consciousness of our nation. Because she sat down, an entire race was able to stand up and challenge the evils of segregation and racism.

On the dreadful day of September 11, 2001, the United States of America was attacked in the most horrific and cowardice fashion. I watched the television in awe and disbelief at the pure chaos and fear that swept not only New York City, Washington D.C. and Pennsylvania; but our entire country as well. I watched hundreds of people running away in sheer terror from the fire filled towers. As others were running away, the firefighters, with their faces fixed like flint, walked right into the heart of the mangled fire filled disasters, not only in New York City, but also in Washington D.C. and in Pennsylvania. They did their jobs, with many losing their lives in the process. Those firefighters realized that was their moment to do what they had spent all those hours training to do -- SAVE LIVES!

86,400

My friend each day we are blessed with eighty-six thousand four hundred seconds. What we do with each of those "moments" is totally up to us. Unfortunately many people waste their moments complaining, worrying, or stressing about things in which they have no control over or simply refuse to take action on the things that they can change. Use your moments and seize each one. Enjoy the moments because in a moment, life can change quickly and sometimes drastically. Each day, each moment you and I have a choice on what we will do with it.

I can never go back to that moment in the airport with my son and do that over again. But what you and I can both do is to make sure that we cherish the moments that matter most. Slow down and smell the roses of life instead of speeding through life, blowing the roses right off their stems. You live only once. Enjoy the moments and seize them because moments are the stuff that life is made of!

1. What could you do to make sure that you are enjoying life's precious moments?

2. What's preventing you now from enjoying moments?

Your Definition of Success Is the Only One That Matters

*"One of the most common mistakes and one of the costliest is
thinking that success is due to some genius, some magic,
something or other which we do not posses."*
-Maltbie Babcock (1858-1901)

In 1923 the world's wealthiest men at that time met at Chicago's Edge-water Beach Hotel. They all possessed power, fame and amazing fortunes. In fact it was said that at that particular time they had power over more money than the total amount within the United States Treasury. These individuals were powerful and in many peoples' eyes, ultra successful. But were they really successful? Look at who they were and their final outcomes:

- *Charles Schwab-* president of the largest independent steel company-died broke.
- *Arthur Cutten-* greatest of the wheat speculators-died abroad, insolvent (unable to pay debts)
- *Richard Whitney-* president of the New York Stock Exchange-died just after release from Sing Sing prison.
- *Albert Fall-* member of the U.S. presidents cabinet-was pardoned from prison so that he could die at home.
- *Jess Livermore-* greatest "bear" on Wall Street-committed suicide.
- *Leon Fraser-* president of the Bank of International Settlements- committed suicide.
- *Ivar Kreuger-* head of the world's greatest monopoly-committed suicide.

(source: Bill Rose, New York Herald Tribune, November 8, 1948).

Our society places a high premium on becoming wealthy, powerful and reaching fame, even though we know that none of that sustains long lasting joy if that's the main goal. We see athletes who demand "more" money even though they are millionaires many times over. We see entertainers constantly raising their fees in the same fashion. We see high paid CEO's going to jail because they were caught doing something illegal to gain more financial power.

There is nothing wrong with becoming wealthy, powerful and famous; many of these individuals use that leverage for the betterment of mankind. But if those things become the main objective, problems will occur.

"Success is waking up in the morning, whoever you are, wherever you are, however old or young, and bounding out of bed because there's something out there that you love to do, that you believe in, that you're good at- something that's bigger than you are, and you can hardly wait to get at it again today."
-Whit Hobbs

Delay of Game (Delay of Living)
In American football there is a penalty that can be called against the offense called "Delay of Game". This happens when the offense doesn't get the ball snapped within the allotted time of 40 seconds. Before the penalty occurs you will generally see a lot of movement from the offense and maybe even some confusion, but even with all the movement and activity the ball never gets snapped which brings on the penalty.

Many people live their lives similarly in search of true success. There is a lot of activity but very little action. The first step in knowing your definition of success is to know where you want to go and want to do. Otherwise you're just delaying your life; busy with all sorts of things but never focusing on your desired final outcome.

So What is Success?
In my opinion, "True" success is knowing your purpose and final destination. To many, success is simply exercising their God-given gifts and talents for the betterment of mankind. To others, it's being the best mother or father they can be. Still for some it's serving others by rendering excellent service and receiving a great deal of satisfaction from producing and delivering a fantastic product or service. For some it's simply being healthy. The list could go on and on but the thing that doesn't change is those who are truly successful know their purpose and where they want to go with their life. They replace activity with detailed action.

Keep The Main Thing the Main Thing

Burger King may dabble, putting new and interesting items on their menu, but the Whopper is their main thing. They don't deviate from their purpose in trying to provide pizza, lasagna, or chicken fried rice. They leave those items to other restaurants that specialize in those types of items. Since 1954, Burger King has strived to provide a great burger at a great price for it's customers and they have been very successful in doing just that. *You have to know what "your" main thing is and then do it.*

Accepted Amnesia

Accepted amnesia is simply forgetting the past and moving on towards your desired outcomes. It doesn't mean that the event didn't happen or that you didn't take the lessons learned from the event. It simply means not allowing the event in the past to hinder you from moving forward. Stop sabotaging your future by holding on to a painful past.

Enjoy Today

Live every day, everyday. The good, the bad and the ugly are all a part of living. No matter what comes your way today you have the ability to respond to it in whatever fashion you choose. You cannot help "what" happens; but you can decide "how" you will respond to it.

Make your Blueprint and then be flexible

Very few people are successful at anything the first, second or even third time. But one thing that successful people are successful at initially, is devising a plan towards their desired outcomes. As the saying goes; if you fail to plan than you plan to fail. Even after you have your plans written down and you're on your way, don't be so stubborn and fixated on the plan that you don't allow yourself room to adjust when you approach detours. It would be foolish to continue driving down a street when there are signs warning you of an upcoming bridge that is out. Detours are a fact when it comes to the journey of success. Just reroute your journey and continue on.

17

Life Ends When We Stop Learning

There are two ways that we can get our knowledge-
either we can either buy it or borrow it.
—Benjamin Franklin

The United Negro College Fund's motto, "A mind is a terrible thing to waste," is one with which I wholeheartedly agree. It's a tragedy how many people willingly allow their minds to atrophy. One of the best investments you can make is in your own continued learning. Your local library has thousands of books waiting to unlock life's secrets to all who are willing to learn. The Internet has forever changed the way we can acquire information at breakneck speed. There isn't a single subject that cannot be researched if one has the desire to do so.

Be a Student for Life

The beautiful thing about learning is that the more you learn the more you realize how much you really don't know. My Grandma Beattie is eighty-five years old and she is extremely sharp. Why? Because when she retired years ago she only retired as a nurse she didn't retire her mind. She's still a voracious reader and does crossword puzzles, cooks, cleans, gardens, shops. You name it and Grandma Beattie is still doing it. She knows sports, politics and gets herself around better than most people twenty years her junior. She has made a commitment to continue to sharpen her mind through study and refusing to allow life to pass her by. Grandma Beattie is the epitome of a student for life.

Learn or Get Left Behind

With the rate of knowledge doubling every two or three years in almost every profession, it's imperative that you continue to learn regardless of what field your currently in. Those who are not tenaciously and consistently improving their skills and knowledge will fall behind and eventually be left out and eliminated from opportunities. With enormous lay-offs, declining wages and very little job security, it literally pays to know your stuff!

Ways to Learn

Learn from experience. The best way for you to learn how to actually perform a task is to do it. Repetition is the quickest way to gain experience and familiarity with anything. I remember the first time that I spoke in front of an audience and I literally about passed out. My mouth was dry my palms were sweaty and it felt like I had a mouth full of the thickest peanut butter known to man because it seemed like I could barely open my mouth. But with each presentation, it has become easier for me to do what I do. My experience over the past eleven years has helped me tremendously.

Learn from problems. Think about the last time that you faced a major problem in your life? During that time you probably learned a great deal about yourself. Although problems never feel good; you can learn a great deal.

Learn from your mistakes. When I played college football at Nebraska, I remember watching films after a loss and seeing the areas where we could make major improvements. Although I hate to lose in anything, I can clearly say that I've always learned more from a loss than a win. When you make a mistake, fess up to it and learn from it.

Learn by asking questions. One of the best ways that you can learn is by simply saying, "I don't know". Asking questions is a marvelous way to learn but you must be smart enough to know that you don't know. Curiosity is a key factor in continuing to learn and to grow.

Learn from other people. Everything that I've learned and everything you've learned has come from other people. Through books, movies, conversations and life in general, all that you've learned was learned from others. Make it a point to surround yourself with others who are smarter than you are in various areas. Learn from others within your organization. Learn from your customers. Learn from complaints. Learn from achievements. Learn from everyone.

Learn by teaching. When I taught Sunday school, I made sure I taught my students to the best of my ability. In order to teach effectively, I had to prepare myself through study, research and prayer. As a result I learned a tremendous amount about the topics that we covered. If you look hard enough, you have opportunities to teach someone something everyday!

Learn from criticism. The stoic philosopher Epictetus said, "If evil be spoken of you and it be true, correct yourself; if it be a lie, laugh at it." If the criticism is true, then you have to look at it as a good thing and a blessing. No criticism is ever a pleasant experience. The first thing to do is to consider the source of the criticism and then go from there. But whatever you do, correct what needs to be corrected and disregard the rest that doesn't apply.

Continue learning by reading the books, go to the seminars, listen to the CD's while you're commuting to and from work. Listen to an audio book while you're working out. By doing just these things, you'll amaze yourself at how much you can learn.

Make it a priority to begin building your personal library if you haven't already. The following books are just a sample of ones that have literally changed my life by what I've learned and continue to learn from them:

- *The Bible*
- *The Other 90%* by Robert Cooper
- **The Purpose Driven Life** by Rick Warren
- Anything written by John Maxwell
- *Chasing Daylight* by Erwin Raphael McManus
- Anything by Dan Kennedy (Business growth & development)
- *The Richest Man in Babylon* by George Clason
- Anything by Og Mandino
- *What Makes the Great Great* by Dennis Kimbro
- *Acres of Diamonds* by Russell Conwell
- *CEO of Self* by Herman Cain

18

Reasons Must Be Strong

No one ever excused his or her way to success.
-Dave Del Dotto

Know Your Reasons

In the movie *Men of Honor*, Carl Brashear (played by Cuban Gooding, Jr.) was asked why he wanted to become a U.S. Navy Diver so desperately. His response was, "Because they said I couldn't have it." The power and conviction with which he said that line sent a chill down my spine. If your reason is strong enough, there isn't a man-made force that can impede your progress.

Men of Honor was based on the true story of Carl Brashear, a black U.S. Navy diver who, in 1948, demanded more than merely to be able to serve food in the mess halls aboard Navy ships. He was determined to earn the coveted title of Master Navy Diver, even turning down promotions because they would interfere with his goal.

Finally, after years of determination, frustration, blatant racism and even losing his leg in a salvage mission, Carl Brashear's persistence finally paid off. He became a master diver in June 1970, the first African American to accomplish such a feat.

The reason that Carl Brashear wanted to become a Master Navy Diver was that he simply loved the sea and that everyone told him he couldn't achieve his goal. If your reasons are strong enough, you will absolutely astound yourself on what you could accomplish.

Carl Brashear had strong reasons and indomitable convictions, which fueled his desire to become a Master Navy Diver. What indomitable convictions do you have? If you don't know what they are, take ten minutes to list a few and begin immediately to use them as fuel to reach your desired outcomes.

We Eventually Become Like Those We Spend Time With

Bad company corrupts good character.
-The Bible (1 Corinthians 15:33)

Be Careful Who You Associate With

If you want to fly with the eagles, you have to stop hanging out with the vultures. Vultures have their minds on dead things. Eagles are constantly hunting and soaring high above the clouds. Are you an eagle or a vulture? Eagles have their thoughts and sights on things above, searching for things that are alive. They make their company with the summits of mountains and with the other eagles that are constantly soaring majestically high above. Vultures are able to fly high as well, but they are constantly looking for dead things, things with no life or vigor.

There are people who have eagle characteristics and those who have vulture characteristics. Which set of characteristics do you have? These two types of people look at life from two totally different perspectives.

Characteristics of Eagle Personalities:
- They look for life in every situation.
- They tend to hang out with other eagles, which have a positive outlook on life, are goal oriented, and have deep concern for others, well being.
- They refuse to associate with dead and lifeless people or those who are always negative and cynical.
- They enjoy the present view of deep relationships and satisfying careers while taking steps towards their goals and dreams.

Characteristics of Vulture Personalities:
- They thrive on the misfortune of others because they enjoy dead things such as gossip and negativity.
- They are often cynical and associate with other vultures, who also thwart anything productive and lively.
- They are strong-willed in seeing that everyone around them suffers.

Which characteristics do you find yourself displaying most often?

Which one of these characteristics best describes the people you associate with?

My advice is to ditch the vultures and begin flying with the eagles. Why feast on the dead and depressing things in life when you can enjoy a life that's full of possibilities? The choice is yours.

Your Strengths Are What Get You Through

"A true friend knows your weaknesses but shows you your strengths; feels your fears but fortifies your faith; sees your anxieties but frees your spirit; recognizes your disabilities but emphasizes your possibilities."
-William Arthur Ward

During the 1990's, the Nebraska Football team was one of the most dominant teams in the history of college football. Under Head Coach Tom Osborne, Nebraska managed to physically dominate and dismantle the opposing team using what some considered an archaic or old-fashioned style offense called "option football".

The option offense was a thing of beauty. If executed properly, any given play could go the distance for a touchdown. The early 1990's was a time when many top college teams were going to an offense that featured a passing attack, otherwise known as the West Coast Offense. Coach Osborne believed in his team's strengths; therefore, he engineered an offense to suit his philosophy and best utilized the "strengths" of the players on his team.

The national media, pundits, fans, regularly questioned his philosophy and his refusal to join the me-too ranks of college footballs elite. He understood his strengths and played to them and as a result he won National Championships in 1994, 1995, and in 1997 (and was only a play or so away from winning a fourth in 1993).

During our football practices in the early 1990's at Nebraska, we focused on our strength of running the football for the majority of the practice. We practiced passing too, but we knew passing was not our strong suite - so why spend 80% or even 50% of your time working on a weakness?

Unfortunately many organizations, companies and individuals commit this very mistake. They focus on their weaknesses spending resources, time and effort on improving in an area that will never equal that of their strengths. Meanwhile, their areas of strength suffer and even lay dormant for long periods of time while they tinker away in areas that will never render them the success or efficiency that they desire.

41

Celebrate the Great Plays First!

I had the awesome privilege of coaching my son's young football team for two years and it was AWESOME! I made it a point to have as much fun with these young five and six-year-olds as possible. We only practiced once a week and it was usually 30 minutes before our games.

I made it a point to always celebrate the great plays first and show them their mistakes last. When parents receive their children's report cards, all too often they immediately question the young man or woman about the D's and F's and almost ignore the two B's and three A's and possibly the C's that were formerly D's and F's.

This happens throughout the offices of corporate America as well. Sales managers too often look at the ways to improve their sales force by looking at the weakest areas instead of cultivating the areas of strengths within their team.

Highlights vs. Red Laser Chew Out Sessions

The best people in any profession or career focus the majority of their time on their strengths, not their weaknesses. The best teams, athletes, business people constantly play over in their minds the times that they were absolutely brilliant while engaged in their craft and make every effort to duplicate the same results.

You also have those who focus painstakingly on every negative part of their performance, sales presentation, results on an exam, etc. Instead of taking note of their weaknesses and doing what they can to manage them, they actually spend time, effort, and resources on the weakness as if they're strengths. During my football days in college, I remember having to watch films on Mondays of Saturday's game. Fortunately, I had a coach who understood the total waste of time by using one of those red laser pens that show up on the screen to point out every tick tack area of weakness. Sure, he made us understand how we had to improve in areas in order to be successful, but he understood the power of spending the lions share of our preparation time on STRENGTHS, not weakness.

Remember that highlights help you duplicate your desired performance. You feel better watching yourself or mentally going over areas of your strengths. In stark contrast is the mental and even physical anguish you can experience by focusing on the times where you blew it as a result of spending too much time fixated on your weaknesses.

Do What You Do!

I often tell audiences that if your current career is one that you are not passionate about then you are going to have major regrets later in life. I didn't go to college to get a job. Heck, I could have landed a decent job without going to college. I went to college to find out what my passion was. I wanted to study different areas to see what I really enjoyed doing and that I could be passionate about everyday.

During my last two years of college I begin to do some speaking for local youth groups and I absolutely loved it. I was always nervous before each one of them (I still get nervous before I speak no matter what the crowd size is) but the sheer euphoria I felt and still feel before an audience is almost indescribable.

You must figure out what your strengths are and then do those things. Do what you do! Taking the time to truly identify what your strengths are and then acting upon them could be life changing in many ways.

1. Identify the things, personally & professionally, that you do well and do more of them.

2. How do you feel when you are engaged in activities that play to your strengths?

3. How do you feel when you are engaged in activities that you are weak in? Why not manage weaknesses and focus on your strengths?

Friends are Important Parts of Our Lives

A real friend sticks closer than a brother.
-Proverbs 18:24

Think for a moment what your life would be like without your friends? Think about the trips to the mall, sporting events, coffee shop, hunting, fishing, and golfing without those whom you call your friends?

When I'm on the road and if my schedule permits I get a few holes of golf in at one of the local golf clubs. I've been fortunate to be able to play some pretty nice golf courses. Although some of the golf courses are beautiful and breathtaking, it's never as much fun without sharing the experience with some of my good friends. Experiencing life with friends is one of many treats in this life.

A few tips on strengthening existing friendships:

1. Tell Them
Don't ever assume that your friends "know" that you care and appreciate them. Tell them regularly how much you value and appreciate them. Tell them how much depth and meaning that they add to your life. To often we wait until something tragic happens before we voice our love and appreciation to those close to us. Tell them how much you care while they can hear it and appreciate it.

2. Ask Them
Let me warn you that taking this step requires your friendship to be fairly strong. This definitely is not something that all friends could do but it should be one that all friendships eventually can do.

Make it a point to ask your friends how you can be a better friend to them. Ask them what they would like you to do more or less of. Ask them to be completely honest with you. This is powerful because it takes the friendship to another level, away from the shallow stuff and into the real areas of meaning and significance.

3. Show Them

There are literally millions of ways that you can display your appreciation and love for your friends. You could send them a "handwritten" card in the mail (instead of a quick email -- nothing wrong with this but it's terribly overused). You could invite them over for dinner and "serve" them their favorite dish or simply take them out to their favorite eatery and enjoy good food and conversation. Take the time to show them and then what you tell them will mean even more.

A Few Tips on Dealing with Difficult Friendships

In order to build true lasting friendships it takes time, energy, and a lot of trust. Life is short and it's extremely precious. In today's crazy and chaotic world we all look for some sense of consistency and sincerity in our close relationships. Unfortunately, those who we trust the most can also hurt us on a deeper level. Dealing with difficult friendships is stressful, painful and about as fun as going to the dentist for a root canal.

According to friendship expert Dr. Jan Yager, there are twenty-one characteristics that usually accompany those friendships/relationships that tend to be difficult. In her book, *When Friendships Hurt*, Dr. Yager also makes the point that any one of the listed characteristics could be present in your life as well.

1. The Promise Breaker - Constantly disappoints you or breaks promises.

2. The Taker - Borrows and fails to return something precious or valuable to you.

3. The Double-Crosser - Betrays you big time.

4. The Risk Taker - Puts you in harm's way because of illegal or dangerous behavior.

5. The Self-Absorbed - Never has time to listen to you.

6. The Cheat - Lies, or steals your romantic partner.

7. The Discloser - Betrays your confidence.

8. The Competitor - Excessively combative with you and wants what you have - relationships, job, possessions.

9. The One-Upper - Always one up on you.

10. The Rival - Wants whatever you have and may try to take it from you.

11. The Faultfinder - Overly critical.

12. The Downer - Always negative, critical, and sad, and makes you feel that way too.

13. The Rejecter - Dislikes you and lets you know it.

14. The Abuser - Verbally, physically, or sexually abuses you.

15. The Loner - Would rather be alone than with a friend.

16. The Blood Sucker - Overly dependent.

17. The Therapist - Needs to analyze everything and give you advice.

18. The Interloper - Overly involved in your life.

19. The Copy Cat - Imitates you.

20. The Controller - Needs to dominate you or the friendship.

21. The Caretaker - Needs to be a friend's keeper, mother or nursemaid, rather than an equal.

By no means am I, or the author of that book, insinuating that you immediately terminate the friendship if it displays any or all of the above characteristics. Each of us at one time or another has displayed many of these unpleasant characteristics towards friends. However, the warning exists to avoid having these things become permanent fixtures in your friendships.

Terminating Friendships

Ending a friendship can be extremely painful and unbelievably joyful at the same time. I have not had to end many friendships during my lifetime and for that I'm extremely thankful. There is one that stands out for me that was very painful. Nevertheless, I thank God that it happened and as a result, I'm a better person. When you're ending a friendship you must be firm, factual and very clear. Most importantly, do it with respect and class. If you don't feel that you can be respectful in person then it's probably best to send a letter rather than subject yourself to a possible blow-up in person. In my opinion, face to face is the best way to do this. However, because of certain circumstances, that may not be possible. Remember, be firm, factual and respectful!

Restoring Friendships

Restoring a friendship can be just as painful and arduous as terminating one. In order to restore a friendship after a transgression, it takes both parties. Restoration doesn't necessarily mean that your friendship will be like it was. In fact, very few ever get back to where they were before the transgression occurred. In my case, I heard the other person out, explained to them why it hurt me, forgave them, wished them continued success and left. Restoration is possible and can be very rewarding.

Life is a Contact Sport

It is time for us all to stand and cheer for the doer, the achiever -- the one who recognizes the challenges and does something about it.
-Vince Lombardi

Growing up in Lincoln, Nebraska, the major source of all entertainment was college football. During each home football game, you could drive downtown towards Memorial Stadium and encounter thousands of fans converging on the nearby stores and restaurants, eagerly anticipating the start of another Husker Football Game. Once the game began, the stadium would fill to capacity with over 76,000 screaming spectators, ready to watch their beloved Huskers play.

I was blessed to have had the opportunity to play football for Nebraska in the early nineties, and it was surreal to run out of the locker room to be greeted by the huge roar of excitement. Although watching the event was fun, participating in it was unbelievable. It's the same with life. Watching life can be fun, but allowing yourself to become nothing but a spectator is a tragedy.

As a participant in life, you have sacrifices to make, goals to reach, obstacles to overcome, and commitments to keep. But as a result of your labor the rewards are priceless. In 1994, Nebraska won college football's most coveted award, the National Championship. I was fortunate enough to be a member of that awesome team. Each participant on the team was given a beautiful, massive, diamond-studded National championship ring. Although Nebraska has some of the best college football fans in all the land, not a single one of the 76,000 who filled that stadium up for every home game during the 1994 season was awarded a ring. Only the participants on the team received one.

Refuse to be a Spectator

To go from spectator to participant, you simply decide to no longer settle for watching your life pass you by. As a spectator you will never know how it feels to perform under pressure while your heart is pounding and the roof of your mouth is so dry that you can hardly breathe. Spectator's can never understand how a badly it hurts to lose a closely contested competition. The spectator cannot grasp the sheer agony of defeat nor the euphoria of seeing all of your hard work finally payoff.

Those who leave the safety of the stands to participate in this awesome event called life qualify for the championships that life has to offer. Are you a spectator or participant in life?

> *"The credit belongs to the person who is actually in the arena; whose face is marred by dust and sweat and blood; who strives valiantly; who errs and comes up short again and again; who knows the great enthusiasm, the devotion, and spends himself or herself in a worthy cause; who at best knows in the end the triumph of high achievement; and at worst, at least fails while daring greatly; so that his or her place shall never be with those cold and timid souls who know neither victory nor defeat."*
> *- President Theodore Roosevelt*

23
You Never Know Unless You Ask

Others have seen what is and asked why. . .I have seen
what could be and asked why not.
-Robert F. Kennedy

Imagine what your life, your relationships, and your business would look like if you really asked for what you wanted. It's a real tragedy that many people just live their lives accepting whatever life hands them in all areas of their lives.

Do What My Boys Do
When I am at the store with my boys, picking up a few things, they never fail to ask me to buy them something. It doesn't matter what store we are in or how much the item costs. They ASK!! In fact, they usually just don't ask me one time or for one thing. It's multiple requests of "Daddy, can you buy me this? . . ." and "Daddy can you buy me that?..." Daddy, Daddy, Daddy!

My young son's requests serve as a constant reminder that you must ask for what you want. You *may* not get what you ask for but you will *never* get what you don't ask for (unless it's a cold or something).

If you're a married man, then you asked for your wife's hand in marriage; if you have a job, you asked for the job. If you've ever been lost, you've asked for directions (unless you allowed your ego to get in the way of acknowledging that you were lost). The point is, we all have asked for something before. For some reason, we tend to stop asking what it is we truly desire and long for in life.

Stop Being Afraid of the Word NO!
As I mentioned above, my kids have no problem hearing the word "no." In fact, when they hear "no" it's almost as if they didn't hear my response. Kids truly believe that "no" is just a "yes" waiting to happen. If you're already not getting what you truly desire out of life then what do you have to lose by asking? You have absolutely nothing to fear!

Become Worthy

If you're having trouble asking for something because you don't feel that you're worthy of the request, then do something about it. If you're in sales and thinking of asking your area manager for a raise but your numbers are not where they could be, first go out and do a lights out job in getting your numbers above and beyond expectations. Before you ask, make sure that you've done all you can do on your part to make yourself a worthy candidate of receiving that which you asked for.

Be the Example

If you desire more, then give more. Be the epitome and the example of the very thing that you desire. To receive better service, then give the best service! If you're asking for the attitude in your office to be positive then you need to be the example of a positive attitude. If you're asking for complete integrity in the office, at home or on the team then you be the example of unquestionable integrity. Be that which you desire!

Choose to want more than to merely exist. God has given each of us a tremendous amount of potential and ability. It's up to us to tap into the deep reservoir of talent that lies within each of us and use it. If you ask life for anything less, that's exactly what you'll get. Ask for what you want and then take action and go get it!

Asking is the beginning of receiving.
Make sure you don't go to the ocean with a teaspoon.
At least take a bucket so the kids won't laugh at you.
-Jim Rohn

Life Can Get Messy

The purpose of life, after all, is to live it, to taste experience
to the utmost, to reach out eagerly and without fear for
newer and richer experience.
–Eleanor Roosevelt

Enjoy Tripping Over the Tractors

When my boys were younger, they loved toy tractors. Each morning, as I made my way down the stairs, I had to remind myself to watch where I stepped, or it could be deadly. There were many times when I had to use my failing, yet still adequate, football agility to avoid a back-breaking fall during one of my midnight walks to the bathroom. One night, as I was walking through the kitchen, I wasn't so lucky and I stubbed my toe on one of my boys' small metal tractors. It hurt so badly that I thought I was dreaming, until my big toe began to throb. But as much pain as I was in, I could only squeeze out a painful chuckle as I thought about how much my little guys loved their tractors and dump trucks and the thousand other toys that litter our house.

As I sat in the kitchen watching my big toe throb, my mind went back to when each of my boys was born and the joy and elation that my wife and I were blessed to experience. I remember buying footballs before they were even home from the hospital and gathering little toy dump trucks and Hot Wheel cars, dreaming about the day when they would be running through the house, being rambunctious little boys.

That particular night, I realized the joy of tripping over tractors and high stepping over Lego forts. All of this madness, as frustrating as it can sometimes be, is a sign of life in my home. I've come to enjoy coming home when my house is in utter chaos from my little guys running all over the place, allowing their imaginations to turn our living room couch into their operation headquarters, with pillows piled almost to the ceiling. I love the fact that I have several hand-painted pictures with jelly stains on the sides in my office. I loved the times they'd come running to tell me that they actually went to the bathroom in the bathroom instead of in their pants or somewhere else for that matter. My heart skips a beat when I return home from a trip and I see my little troopers running to see me, and they say that one word that's sweet music to my ears, "DADDY!"

You see, I don't mind tripping over the tractors anymore, because it's a sign of life in my home-those little red tractors constantly remind me to enjoy my family and friends. Life is too precious to get upset about the little tractors in our lives.

When you find yourself getting all bent out of shape over the little things of life, pause for a minute and be grateful for them. Those little things are what help you realize that you're living and that you're alive. We can easily miss the awesome message within the mess.

Your Dreams Are Up to You

I'll do my dreaming with my eyes wide open,
and I'll do my looking back with my eyes closed.
—Tony Arata

As a kid I would often dream of running out of the tunnel at Memorial stadium right before the big kick-off and hearing the blare of the band along with the cheers of the crowd. I would imagine myself catching the winning touchdown to beat the Oklahoma Sooners for the Big Eight Championship.

I eventually had the chance to play for Nebraska, but I only had one career catch and it wasn't for the Big Eight Championship nor was it against Oklahoma. Rather, it was against the Missouri Tigers and we were already winning the game rather handedly before I even got on the field. Sure, I was a bench warmer but I was a kid in a candy store each Saturday that I lived my childhood dream by running out of the tunnel in front of 76,000 screaming fans.

"Ain't no man can avoid being average, but there ain't no man got to be common" -Satchel Paige

Conformity Kills Dreams

It never ceases to amaze me how many people allow their dreams to die because they fear what others will say about them; so they conform. Conformity is simply doing what those around do so you will not deviate from the group.

It's a scenario that plays out everyday in the hallways of our schools and the corporate boardrooms as well.

Author and Speaker Dr. Dennis Kimbro says, "Failure is not the opposite of success; conformity is." I couldn't agree more. Many people have hundreds of ideas just bursting within them but allow the evil laws of conformity to cheat them out of all sorts of rewards and satisfaction.

What you do today determines where you will be tomorrow. What you put into your mind will determine what comes out of your mouth.

No matter what you do, it's all up to you. Only you can decide to decide, only you can say enough is enough, only you can read the books, go to the seminars, listen to the CD's and tapes for professional and personal development. Only you can go to bed at night, thinking about your goals and dreams, only you can jump out of bed ready to make your vision a reality. Only you can plan your work and work your plan.

Five Steps towards Realizing your Dreams

1. **Quit:** Quit allowing negative people, surroundings, and feelings to dictate and determine your life.

2. **Focus on what you can become:** Begin focusing on the ideal you. Don't focus on what you currently don't have. Utilize the assets and talents that you currently have and use them to the best of your abilities. Focus on your strengths and continue to cultivate and foster them to lead you in the direction that you seek to go.

3. **Take CRAZY ACTION:** Crazy Action is when you begin taking CRAZY BOLD steps towards your objectives. Not crazy as in out of your mind but crazy as beyond anything you've ever attempted before. For some it's simply getting up thirty minutes earlier to plan your day. For others it's finally gathering up enough nerve and boldness to leave a dead end job and strike out on your own or go for something that better fits your talents.

4. **Write down your vision:** A Japanese saying is :*"Vision without action is a daydream and action with without vision is a nightmare."* Take the time to write down what your vision is and what you will have to do to see it come to fruition.

5. **Work your plan one day at a time:** Take each day as it comes and get the most from it. Don't allow your mind to wander too far ahead. There is nothing wrong with planning for the future, but don't get so fixated with the future that you neglect living in the moment.

Sometimes It's Reasonable to Be Unreasonable

I'm a big fan of dreams. Unfortunately, dreams are our first casualty in life. People seem to give them up, quicker than anything, for a "reality".
–Kevin Costner

You Must Be Unreasonable

In December 2002, a Cuban immigrant secretly climbed underneath the landing gear of a Boeing 747 airplane and remained there for over four hours as the plane exceeded heights of over 30,000 feet and traveled through below-zero temperatures. After the plane landed in a Canadian airport, personnel spotted a man staggering out from under the airplane and they quickly apprehended him.

Let's think about this for a moment. Upon telling his friends and family that he was going to ride underneath a Boeing 747 for over four hours in below-zero temperatures at over 30,000 feet until he arrived in Canada, do you suppose any of them responded by saying, "Hey, that sounds reasonable, go for it." I think it's safe to say that he didn't tell too many people about his choice, because I'm sure they would have responded with "ARE YOU CRAZY!?"

By no means do I applaud this man for such an insane act, but you have to admire the man's determination to make it to freedom in Canada. This man chose not only to be unreasonable when it came to reaching his goal of freedom, but borderline insane! Why does North America and other parts of the free world have those who will risk life and limb to live there? Because of the freedom!

In America, I enjoy all sorts of freedoms that I often take for granted everyday. Famous speaker and philosopher Jim Rohn says, "You never hear anyone say, 'If I could only make it to Poland, then I could really accomplish my goals."

In America, and other parts of the free world we have become too reasonable when it comes to the things that we really desire. Walt Disney was unreasonable when he looked out at a canvassing swamp in South Florida, only to see his unreasonable dream vividly pictured in his mind.

That vivid picture is very much a reality today.

Each time I sit in the seat of a massive Boeing 747 airplane as it races down the runway, I think about how unreasonable the Wright Brothers must have been. When I bring home a bucket of piping hot chicken from Kentucky Fried Chicken, I can't help but think how unreasonable Colonel Sanders had to have been after his now-famous recipe was turned down close to a thousand times. Oprah. Need I say more? Her name is so iconic it needs no explanation. Raised in the hard and unhealed South, enduring family hardships and constantly battling sexism and racism, she ended up as the most popular T.V. talk show host in the history of television.

None of these famous names relied on reason to reach their goals. They had to choose to be unreasonable and believe in the power of their visions. Do you want to achieve your dreams? Then make a deal with yourself to be unreasonable!

1. Are you too reasonable about your goals and dreams and the life that you desire?

2. If God was to have told anyone about his awesome plan of creating such a magnificent creation as planet earth, they would have told him he was being unreasonable. I believe that's why He created man after He created earth. Do you let others dictate your dreams and aspirations? If so, Why?

It's Impossible to Live a Good Life without Integrity

Real integrity stays in place whether the
test is adversity or prosperity.
-Charles Swindoll

Enron, Worldcom, and Adelphia are just a few of the casualties resulting from a widespread lack of integrity we have witnessed in Corporate America in the past few years. These companies, along with many others, sacrificed their integrity for prosperity, and the consequences were catastrophic.

Because a few individuals put their integrity on the sale rack and reaped temporary millions, thousands of people who worked for these greedy giants suffered terrible financial losses. Hundreds, if not thousands, of individuals' retirement accounts, which had taken years to build up, were wiped out in a matter of days as these companies' stocks hit rock bottom.

In the movie, *The Legend of Bagger Vance*, there is a scene where Rannulph Junah, played by Matt Damon, is participating in a closely contested golf match. The match had gone into the night with only the headlights from fans cars providing any sort of lighting to the players. In this particular scene, Rannulph is removing some debris away from his golf ball but in doing so it caused his ball to move. It moved so little that no one even noticed. Well, no one except himself and his young caddie, "Hardy," played by J. Michael Moncrief. Right there, with the match on the line, Rannulph's integrity was being tested.

So the ball moved, no problem right? Wrong! In the game of golf, the ball that is in the fairway cannot be moved in this situation and a one-stroke penalty must be administered. Rannulph Junah's young caddie couldn't believe that Rannulph was actually going to penalize himself one-stroke when no one else saw what happened.

The young caddie would learn a powerful lesson that day. After listening to Hardy plead and beg Rannulph not to report the infraction because no one had saw the ball move, Rannulph responds with one of the most powerful statements in the entire movie. He tells the young caddie that it was wrong and dishonest because "I saw it move"!

Within that small statement is the epitome of integrity. Integrity does not depend on who did or didn't see you. In doesn't matter if the lights are on or off. A person of integrity calls his or her own fouls. Integrity is what you do and what you are when you're the only person around.

From his book, *Up From Slavery*, Booker T. Washington describes meeting an ex-slave:

"I found that this man had made a contract with his master, two or three years previous to the Emancipation Proclamation, to the effect that the slave was to be permitted to buy himself, by paying so much per year for his body; and while he was paying for himself, he was to be permitted to labour where and for whom he pleased.

Finding that he could secure better wages in Ohio, he went there. When freedom came, he was still in debt to his master some three hundred dollars. Notwithstanding that the Emancipation Proclamation freed him from any obligation to his master, this black man walked the greater portion of the distance back to where his old master lived in Virginia, and placed the last dollar, with interest, in his hands.

In talking to me about this, the man told me that he knew that he did not have to pay his debt, but that he had given his word to his master, and his word he had never broken. He felt that he could not enjoy his freedom till he had fulfilled his promise."

What do you get for living a life of integrity?

1. A ***solid reputation*** is a direct result of conducting your personal and professional life with respect, passion and most importantly, integrity. No amount of money can restore a reputation to the point it was before the offense took place.

2. You'll have a ***group of people*** who trust you in any circumstances, with any person, anywhere. Integrity is not determined by any "external" circumstances. Integrity is on the inside. When your life speaks of integrity, people not only listen, but they tend to follow as well.

3. ***Peace of mind*** also encompasses the lives of those who have made a conscious choice to live a life of integrity. Although

there may be chaos going on around them they still have mental peace because they know that at no time did they compromise their most important asset in order to calm the storms.

Can your integrity be bought? Do you bend the truth for quick gain? How much would it take for you to sell out to the lies and corruption that are so readily available to those looking for a shortcut? Remember, Judas sold Jesus out for only thirty pieces of silver. What's your asking price?

1. Is there anything in your life today that could cause someone to question your integrity? Remember, the worst place for a question mark is after the word integrity.

2. How can you shore up your life, personally and professionally, to make sure that you are above reproach?

28

You Can't Swim Very Far with Floaties On

You've got to go out on the limb sometimes,
because that's where the fruit is.
-Will Rogers

Take Risks

It's amazing how much kids can teach you about life if you only pay attention to them. My oldest son, Aden, was at our neighbor's swimming pool during the summer of 2002 with my youngest son, Keenon, and a friend, Jacob, who lived across the street. Aden was four at the time, Keenon was two, and Jacob was nearly two. It wasn't just hot outside, it was smoking HOT, so the water felt exceptionally refreshing this particular day. I was having a great time talking with Jacobs's parents, Kurt and Dawn, while the boys were swimming.

Kurt and Dawn had been taking Jacob to swimming lessons for a period of time and he was like a minnow in the water. This kid was all over the place. I couldn't believe how well he could swim, and he wasn't even two years old yet! Jacob began climbing up the ladder on the side of the pool and then jumping into the water and swimming to his Dad. Little Jacob showed no fear! In the meantime, my wife, Brooke, and I were also watching Aden. He was bobbing up and down in the water with his floaties around his arms, helping him stay afloat. Aden was watching little Jacob jump in and out of the water and swimming circles around all of us without floaties on to hinder him. Never mind that Jacob had taken lessons and spent a lot more time in the water then he had. Aden's confidence in his own swimming abilities grew each time he saw Jacob plunge into the water and swim around. Finally, Aden couldn't stand it any longer. He floated over to my wife and whispered in her ear, "Mommy, can you take off my floaties?" Brooke took them off, and the rest is history.

Aden began to jump in the pool with no reservations. He had the time of his life that day in the pool. Never again has Aden put on a set of floaties to go swimming. As I thought about this incident later that evening, I began to think about how much more I could enjoy swimming through life towards the opportunities and goals that are out there waiting for me.

As adults we are often the ones wearing the floaties. Floaties of fear, anxiety, helplessness, anger, hatred, and all the other emotions that impede our progress to true freedom and exploration of all that life has to offer. That evening in the pool, Aden's confidence grew in his own abilities because he saw someone else doing something that he desired to do. No matter what it is that we desire to accomplish, we can always look for models and examples of others who are doing that very thing. In order to really go after what you really want in life, you only need to do one thing -- remove the floaties.

1. What floaties are you wearing that could be hindering you in the pursuit of your goals?

2. What is the worst thing that could happen if you actually took them off?

3. Whatever is holding you back, decide today to live floatie free!

Life Is Too Short to Spend Forty Hours a Week Doing Something You Hate

I never did a day's work in my life. It was all fun.
-Thomas Edison

It's sad and somewhat amazing how many people destroy their weekends because they are dreading the fact that Monday is inching closer by the hour. There are millions of people that hit the alarm clock each morning, stricken with anxiety because they don't want to face another classroom filled with students, another day confined to an office cubicle, another business flight to Chicago, another shift at the factory, another day of making sales presentations, another morning in court, another meeting with the board of directors…the list could go on and on.

Friend, life doesn't have to be this way. Let me let you in on a little secret that could yield you tremendous peace of mind. If you are not happy with your career, do something else. Don't you owe it to yourself?

The 9/11 Effect

Do you love your work? Do you get up in the morning excited to tackle another day in your given area? Do you often find yourself daydreaming about what your life could be if you did something else for a living? I encourage you to take seriously the answers to the questions listed above. After 9/11 many people begin to think hard and long about their life and the work that consumed a large chunk of their time. People began to think because 9/11 forced all of us to re-evaluate what our priorities were. The twisted steel and charred debris caused an entire world to stop, listen and ponder.

Change Jobs and Change Your Life

If you're not happy with your current job then it might be in your best interest to make a career change. I'm not saying that if you don't like your job then you should quit with nothing lined up and simply walk away. What I am saying is that if you're not happy with your job and it no longer brings out passion and energy, then you need to seriously evaluate. Life is way too short to spend forty hours a week in a career

63

that no longer provides you with purpose and satisfaction. Your life will change if you make a well-thought out change. We only have 86,400 seconds a day and we will never get that time back. I have friends who decided that enough was enough and made changes in their careers that literally changed their lives. They reported having more energy, passion and more importantly, peace of mind.

What's holding you back? Remember that putting things off holds no guarantees that you actually get the opportunity to fulfill what you're putting on hold. Tomorrow is not guaranteed for any of us. Consider this very seriously because the only guarantee that you have is this moment.

1. What do you really want professionally? What will you have to do in order to get it?

2. If you love your job great. How can you make it even more rewarding?

3. If you hate your job and despise the drive each morning then what are you waiting for?

4. Begin by searching your heart and mind. Ask God to give you the confidence and plan to take steps towards the career you've always wanted. Remember it's going to take time and sheer determination along with a lot of hard work, you will not regret it.

30

You Already Have What It Takes

Use the gifts that God has already given you and soar!
-Aaron Davis

Believe in Your Abilities

In the bible, there is a conversation in which God is attempting to show Moses that he already has what it takes to carry out the great task of leading the children of Israel out of captivity. God asked Moses what it was he had in his hand, to which Moses replied, "A staff."

With that staff, and using the talents and gifts that he already had, Moses would lead an entire nation out of captivity. Moses had no idea that God would use him and that lowly staff to orchestrate the greatest mass exodus in human history.

There Are No Ordinary Things in Life

The things in your life that you may consider as simply ordinary can be used to do something extraordinary! Employ your "ordinary" talents and utilize your gifts and abilities.

The world is full of ordinary people who have done extraordinary things. The best example I have is my father. He moved from Pittsburgh, Pennsylvania to Lincoln, Nebraska in the early 1960's so that he could raise a family away from the mean streets of Pittsburgh. He didn't know anyone except his brother, who was stationed in Nebraska for the military. No education, no connections and he did it during the heat of the civil rights movement. Ordinary move for an American man some may say, but as a young black male with no education, moving clear across the country; in my humble opinion, would be classified as EXTRAORDINARY!

It's amazing what could happen in your life if you would employ your "ordinary" talents and utilize your gifts and talents. Russell Conwell discussed in his timeless classic, *Acres of Diamonds,* you need to begin using the tools and talents you already possess -- begin digging where you are. The search for significance and for purpose could end for many if they would only look at what God has already blessed them with.

1. You already have the raw materials to begin a life you've always wanted. Today, take ten minutes to do an inventory of your assets. What did you find out?

2. How can you use your assets to begin to move towards your true purpose in life?

Life is Full of Pain, but It's Also Full of Choices

*God has given us two incredible things; absolutely awesome
ability and freedom of choice. The tragedy is that, for the
most part, many of us have refused them both.*
-Frank Donnelly

Choose Wisely

There's not a person alive, whether they be eight or eighty, who hasn't experienced some sort of pain. Whether it's a divorce, death of a loved one, job loss, or a troubled teenager, pain affects all of us. Although the source of our pains may differ, the discomfort that accompanies it is universal. God has given each of us an awesome ability, and that is the ability to choose.

Choices Contain *Potential* Power

Everyday, each second, minute and hour you and I have a ton of potential power, the power of choice. I believe it's only potential power because many people put their days and entire lives on auto-pilot without understanding the power of their ability to choose. William James said it best when he said, "The greatest discovery of my generation is that a human being can alter his life by altering his attitude of mind!" Simply put, we can choose our attitudes!

Each choice that we make is either guiding us closer to our desired outcomes or leading us further away. Life only happens to people who don't make choices. People who make choices and then act on them make their life evolve around the choices they make. They understand and harness the power of choice and utilize it to their advantage.

You have the choice to tackle each day with passion and enthusiasm or you can choose to get up with a terrible attitude and make everybody pay for it. You can allow the person who cut you off in traffic to cause you to wave with one finger, or you can just smile or simply ignore it; the choice is ALWAYS yours.

A few things to think about as you make your choices:

1. Be a student of your choices -- don't just make haphazard choices with no thought or time to consider the outcomes.

2. Weigh the Pros and Cons: No matter what you choose, there will always be consequences. Even if you don't choose, you have made the choice to not do anything, and even that has consequences (for example, try ignoring that red light on your car instrument panel warning you of low fuel and you will experience this lesson first hand; I don't recommend you try this).

3. Do it ALREADY! After you think about it and weigh the pros and cons, it's time to do it already! Stop procrastinating and do the thing!

My friend, we live in a time where technology has literally given us infinite choices, but you must choose as if your life depends on it, because it does.

1. How have your past choices caused you to forfeit great opportunities?

2. What would happen to you if you began to think about your daily choices a little more closely?

You Can Learn a Lot by Digging Post Holes

Character is what you really are deep down and
it never depends on circumstances.
-Aaron Davis

Make Sure Your Post is Solid

One day, I was helping my brother-in-law, Bart, set some fence posts on his property. Anyone who has ever manually set fence posts knows how hard this type of work is. When you're digging these holes, you first have to make sure that they are deep enough, and then you place the post in the hole and slowly begin to fill it with dirt, stopping every few minutes to pack the dirt tightly against the post. As we were doing this, Bart stopped and told me something that his Grandpa Beattie had told him a long time ago.

Grandpa Beattie said, "If the post is solid at the bottom, it'll be solid at the top." That statement can relate to one's character in many ways.

When we see men of a contrary character,
we should turn inwards and examine ourselves.
– Confucius

What you possess in the world will be found at the day of your death
to belong to someone else. But what you are will be yours forever.
– Henry Van Dyke

I like to describe character using the following acronym.

C: Courage: It takes courage to remain faithful and hold strong to your convictions.

H: Humility: Solid character is always permeated with humility.

A: Abstain: Stay away from people, places and situations that could tarnish your name.

R: Responsible: People of solid character take responsibility for their lives.

A: Acknowledge: Acknowledging and admitting when you've made a mistake.

C: Choices: Character driven individuals are always thinking about the choices they make in all areas of their lives.

T: Trustworthy: Character driven individuals are totally trustworthy.

E: Empathize: Character driven individuals try to place themselves in the shoes of others to serve and help others more effectively.

R: Relentless: Character driven individuals are relentless at trying to serve as many people as they can. They understand that the greatest thing that people can do for each other is to serve them.

People Can Be Like Termites

Beware of the termites in your life. The people you associate with the most can also be the ones who cause you the most pain on the road to achieving your full potential.
-Aaron Davis

According to betterpestcontrol.com, over 600,000 U.S. homes battle with those pesky critters called termites. The damage they cause is estimated at over $1.5 billion each year. This is said to be more damage than all natural disasters combined. Over 2 million homes are treated each year without the help of insurance because they don't usually offer termite insurance. Though they may be small, termites will eat there way right through the foundation of a house. It's amazing how people can be the same way. I call these types of people P.T.'s (People Termites) since they share many of the same characteristics.

Beware of People Termites
Some people absolutely thrive off ruining other people's hopes and dreams. This type of person is constantly eating away at your confidence and your self-worth, telling you things like, "You could never do that" or "What will everyone think?" or "You're just going to regret it later." Each time you allow yourself to believe these comments, it's another bite that these P.T.'s have taken out of the foundation of your hopes and dreams. If you allow it to continue long enough, your hopes, dreams and desires will eventually fall to the ground, the foundation eaten right out from under them.

Beware of the termites in your life. The subtle comments may seem small and insignificant at the time, but as time passes those things that appeared harmless can be the most destructive.

If you realized how powerful your thoughts are,
you would never think a negative thought.
–Peace Pilgrim

Perform Regular Exterminations in your Life

The best way to perform regular exterminations of those people termites in your life is by taking just a few minutes to think about the types of people you associate with. Which ones are always taking shots at you? Which ones scoff at you when you talk about bettering yourself? Who are those personal & professional associates that hinder you from being all that God has called you to be? Once you identify these people, begin distancing yourself from them.

Unfortunately, some of these people may be living under the same roof as you. In this case, you must confront them sternly and in a very matter of fact manner that you will not tolerate it, each time and EVERY time it occurs! If you don't take yourself seriously, why should anyone else?

Losers Don't Value Fundamentals

The most successful coaches at any level teach the fundamentals.
- John McKay

The late Vince Lombardi was one of the greatest football coaches of all time in the National Football League. In 1958, Lombardi became the head coach of the Green Bay Packers, which, at the time, were considered the laughingstock of the NFL, since they had won only one game the previous season.

Vince Lombardi's training camps were characterized their sheer intensity and his obsession with fundamentals. In fact, Lombardi was said to have begun one of these intense practices by gathering the players around him and, once there was absolute silence, holding up a football and saying the following: "Gentlemen, this is a football." I can only imagine the look of confusion on the faces of the players sitting around their coach; they were probably wondering if he had gone mad

Coach Lombardi promised his players that if they faithfully and tenaciously clung to the fundamentals of the game of football more so than any of their opponents, they would be champions. Three years later, that's exactly what happened. December 31, 1961, Vince Lombardi coached his team to a 37-0 victory over the New York Giants, winning the National Football League Championship. Because of Coach Lombardi's insistence on sticking to the fundamentals, the Packers would go on to win six division titles, five NFL Championships, and the first two Super Bowls.

Focus on The Fundamentals

What are the fundamentals of your profession? Maybe your sales are down and you can't put your finger on the reason. Get back to the fundamentals. Perhaps your planning team is spending too much time planning and not enough time implementing the plans. Get back to the fundamentals. Maybe your relationship with your teenager consists of jeers and shrugs at the morning breakfast & dinner table. Get back to the fundamentals. No matter if it's personal or professional, neglecting the fundamentals always leads to losing.

Three Reasons Why Fundamentals Get Neglected

1. **Success:** Success can be the biggest detriment to long-term sustained growth and achievement. If you ever watch sports you can see this happen all the time. "Iron" Mike Tyson was called the most feared man on the planet when he stepped into a boxing ring. His meteoric rise to boxing prominence during the late eighties and mid nineties almost pales in comparison to his catastrophic fall from the top. After becoming the youngest heavyweight champion of the world at only twenty years old that became the beginning of the end for young Tyson's boxing career. The same hunger, discipline, passion and determination that it took for you to achieve your objectives is the same amount and more that will be required to sustain your level of achievement.

2. **Shortcuts:** Don't get me wrong here. I'm all for finding ways to do things quicker and faster. But quicker and faster should never take the place of doing things right. I fly in a lot of airplanes and love to arrive at my destination on time. In their efforts to make sure that each plane has an on-time departure and arrival it would not be a good idea for the planes to only load up half the luggage of the passengers in order to depart quicker and arrive faster. People often neglect the fundamentals and exchange them for costly and even unethical shortcuts.

3. **Fatigue:** Many companies have a twenty-four hour rule for their employees who make international flights. Why? Because they understand that fatigue and business meetings are not a good mix. Those twenty-four hours allows a person to decompress and more importantly allow their bodies ample time to adjust to the time change so that they can think clearly. If you're tired, it's awful hard to focus on the fundamentals of your profession. REST! REST! REST!

1. List the top three fundamentals of success in your business or industry. Then, do so in your marriage and/or your relationship with your children.

2. How would you rate yourself in adhering to the three top fundamentals in each of the above areas?

3. What could you do today to improve them?

Sometimes You Will Want to Quit

Keep going and the chances are you will stumble on something, perhaps when you are least expecting it. I never heard of anyone stumbling on something sitting down.
-Charles Kettering

Don't Stop Trying in Trying Times

Because he didn't quit, he was able to help raise and provide for six kids with only a ninth-grade education. However, because he didn't quit, through his faith in God and his pit-bull determination, he taught himself to read by studying the best selling book on the shelves, the Bible. Because he didn't stop trying in trying times, he moved his family from the mean streets of Pittsburgh, Pennsylvania in 1963 to the safe haven of Lincoln, Nebraska.

Because he didn't quit, he started his own janitorial business, securing cleaning contracts with some of Lincoln's most profitable businesses. Because he didn't stop trying in trying times, he became the pastor of a small church, where lives are transformed and relationships are forged for eternity. Because Myles Davis didn't stop trying in trying times, he became the man that I proudly call Dad!

Friend, remain strong in trying times, because it's through the torrential storms of life that we come to learn and appreciate life itself.

The Ring That Got Away

In the spring of 1995 I made a decision that I still regret to this day. I quit playing football for one of the most storied college football programs in the history of collegiate sports. I wasn't a superstar or starter but I was a part of something that was very special. I was fortunate and blessed to win one championship as a member of the 1994 team and in 1995 Nebraska became the first football team in years to win back-to-back National Championships. My friend I never received one of those rings from the 1995 season because I quit. I walked away from Football for all the wrong reasons and as a result I missed out on the opportunity to win another championship and be a part of one of the GREATEST teams ever assembled in college football.

I can't tell you how much the regret from that has driven me over the years. I'm relentless and tenacious when it comes to seizing opportunities. My friend, anytime you quit anything for the "wrong" reasons, you will always miss out!

1. How many championship rings (opportunities) have you left behind? What has quitting for the "wrong" reasons cost you in the past?

2. Whenever you feel like quitting something for the wrong reasons, I want you to think about the consequences to yourself, your family and your faith.

We All Have 24 Hours a Day

*We have to live but one day at a time, but
we are living for eternity in that one-day.
-Anonymous*

Don't Wait Another Day

If you knew that you had only two weeks left to live, how would your life change? Would you write that letter to a friend you've been putting off? Would you end a family feud? Would you call up your son or daughter and tell them you were sorry? Maybe you've been putting off a few minor things in your life that, if you just took the time to do them, would make a major impact. Whatever your case may be, just get started doing it. Contrary to popular opinion, time is not on our side.

*The supply of time is a daily miracle. You wake up in the morning and lo! Your purse is magnificently filled with 24 hours of the unmanufactured tissue of the universe of life. It is yours! The most precious of your possessions.
-Arnold Bennet*

Time is Priceless

Voltaire, the famous French infidel, reportedly said to his doctor, "I will give you half of what I'm worth if you can give me six months of life." Things that are plentiful or that can be obtained fairly easily usually carry the least amount of value. For instance, if yachts were the same price as small bass finder boats, yachts would not hold the same prestige and value that they do. If silver and gold were given to us freely, they would not be seen as so valuable. So it is with time.

We all just assume that we have a lot of time to do all the things that we want to do, and that couldn't be further from the truth. Even as you read this, someone just took their last breath somewhere in the world. As you read this, someone was given just a few months to live. Today, somewhere, family and friends paid their last respects to a departed loved one.

First Fifteen

In my opinion, the way a person spends the first fifteen minutes of their day can influence their day in either a positive or negative way. Many people destroy their day before it even starts by getting up late because they were constantly slapping the alarm clock around on the night stand in search of the snooze button. Finally after three or four snooze sessions they jump out of bed, not out of excitement, but because they are going to have just ten minutes to shower, dress, eat and get the kids out to school, walk the dog, empty the trash all before going to class, the office and to make their flight. All of this rushed and stressed activity first thing in the morning only makes a person uneasy, unnecessarily stressed, and definitely not in a productive state of mind.

Use that first fifteen minutes to plan your day while you are calm, fresh and alert. I challenge you to try it for twenty-one days and see if you will not notice a difference in your whole day because you spent the first fifteen planning it!

My friend, we all get the same amount of time each day and we are free to use it as we wish. Though it may seem that you have all the time in the world to do all the things you want to do with your life, you don't! Each of us is only a heartbeat away from meeting our maker. Thank God each day, squeeze every hour, enjoy each minute and moment because remember you can't get any of them back.

1. Do it today! What is the "it" in your life that you have been putting off? The "it" that keeps you up at night and whispers to you throughout the day? What is your "it?"

Two Natural Remedies: Laughter and Tears

The cheapest prescription that you will ever find is a
dose of laughter, a shot of tears and a balm of forgiveness.
-Aaron Davis

Let the Laughter Roll and the Tears Flow

It's been widely reported that the average preschooler laughs about 450 times a day and the average adult laughs about 15 times a day. Of course, we know that preschoolers sometimes laugh at things we may deem inappropriate, but for heavens sake, even if they "get it right" half the time, that's still 225 laughs a day! That's more than fifteen times the amount that the average adult laughs.

My kids, Aden, Keenon and Niya sometimes fall and just start laughing. And no, they don't rush to get up and make sure no one was looking. In fact, they often announce it to the whole neighborhood, "Hey, everybody, I just fell!" In this same situation, the average adult would get up so fast you'd think the ground was poisonous to anyone over the age of twenty.

Lighten up a little and stop taking yourself so seriously. On the flip side, don't forget to cry either. Unfortunately, many still buy into the antiquated notion that "real men" don't cry and that women who cry are unstable. These beliefs are mind boggling to me. Because our society has become so callous and insensitive, crying, which is totally natural and healthy, has become unnatural and a sign of weakness. In reality, it's one of the greatest forms of therapy that God has freely given us.

Let life move you and allow simple everyday moments to tug at your heart. Cry at a good movie, a touching story and song that elicit either love or pain. Just cry and see if it's not therapeutic to your heart and soul.

1. When was the last time you had a good old-fashioned tear-jerking sob session? How did it make you feel after you used up a box of tissues?

2. When was the last time you laughed so hard and so long that it felt like you just finished an abdominal workout? What's stopping you from having a hearty laugh?

3. Hey, stop taking yourself so seriously that you can't laugh and bury those old lies that real men don't cry and only unstable women do. It's really the other way around.

It's Easy to Find Someone to Blame

"The woman you gave me as a companion, she gave me the fruit from the tree, and, yes, I ate it." God said to the Woman, "What is this that you've done?" "The serpent seduced me," she said, "and I ate."
-Genesis 3:12-13

Since Adam blamed Eve and Eve blamed the serpent for their part in the eating the fruit, blame has saturated every area of life. Blame has destroyed companies where CEO's refused to accept responsibility for their own poor leadership and poor decisions. Blame has snatched victory out of the hands of good sports teams because individual players would not accept responsibility for their own lackluster performances choosing instead to point the finger at teammates, coaches, administration, boosters etc. Blame has infiltrated the homes of families where husbands and wives blame each other for their passionless marriages and dysfunctional families. (And by the way, what family isn't dysfunctional in some capacity?) Blame is wreaking havoc everywhere when individuals refuse to accept responsibility for their own actions.

Hold yourself responsible for a higher standard than anybody else expects of you, never excuse yourself.
- Henry Ward Beecher

Take Responsibility

Responsibility is simply taking ownership of your own actions and refusing to make excuses. There is a saying that goes as the following:

Excuses are tools of the incompetent, which create monuments of nothingness, and those who specialize them are seldom good in anything.

People who tend to rely on excuses instead of simply taking responsibility are their own worst nightmare. I remember speaking to a college student who explained to me why he wasn't doing well in a particular class. After listening to him tell me that the professor didn't like him (out of a lecture class of over 200) and that the material covered on the test wasn't covered in the classroom and that the grading system wasn't fair, I finally stopped him. I simply asked him what he was going to do about it. He paused and looked at me like I had spoken to him in a foreign language. You see, the moment we make an excuse for our own lack of success in any given area, our progress is immediately stopped. We are usually much more willing to come up with an alibi than we are to admit that we need to take responsibility for our both our success and our failures.

I continued to explain to the young man that there were a number of things that he could do to better his grade but that he would first have to stop making excuses and creating alibis and start taking responsibility. I suggested that he meet with the professor (which he had never done before) and explain to him his concerns; start asking questions in class if he didn't understand the material presented. I'm not sure if he ever took my advice but I can guarantee this; if he didn't do SOMETHING he was going to continue to get the same dreaded results he had been getting.

Responsibility can save your job, family and even your life if you stop blaming and start taking control of your life and actions.

I don't read many email forwards unless I know who sent them and the nature of them but this one below was pretty good.

First, plant 3 rows of peas:
- Patience
- Positive thinking
- Persistence

Next, plant 3 rows of squash:
- Squash excuses
- Squash blame
- Squash criticism

Then, plant 3 rows of lettuce:
- Let us be responsible
- Let us be trustworthy
- Let us be ambitious

Finish, with 3 rows of turnip:
- Turn up when needed
- Turn up with a smile
- Turn up with confidence

Here are three quick tips to help you out of the web of blame:

1. If you mess up, fess up! Take responsibility for your mistakes and learn from them.

2. Keep your blame radar in good working condition. Blame is very subtle, so make sure to keep tabs on your emotions.

3. Think about the pain before you blame. Before your start blaming someone else, think about the potential pain that you may cause others and yourself. In some cases, the damage can be irreparable.

Teamwork Always Gets You Further

Talent wins games, but teamwork and
intelligence wins championships.
-Michael Jordan

Can you show me a football team that can win a single game with only a running back? How about a basketball team that can win a game with only a center? Can a company grow and sustain growth without a team of intelligent and dedicated professionals? There's little hope for a student in reaching his or her full potential without a nurturing mentor and guidance. No one does anything without a team. NOBODY! My friend, even Jesus had twelve disciples to spread the Gospel. The president has a cabinet and the head coach has assistants.

Great Teams have Great Team Players

The Boston Celtics of the 1950's and 1960's, the Los Angeles Lakers in the 1980's, the Chicago Bulls in the 1990's. All of these basketball teams had remarkable dynasties during those years. The Celtics during the 60's had Bill Russell, the Lakers had Magic Johnson, and the Bulls, of course, had arguably the best player to ever play the game in Michael Jordan. Although each of these players were excellent and extremely gifted, none of them would have won a single championship on their merits alone. Each of these players had to use their talent to benefit the whole team. Each of these players came to realize that no matter how well they did individually, the team would only be successful if their individual efforts complemented or raised the level of the other four guys on the basketball court.

Coming together is a beginning, staying together is
progress, and working together is success.
-Henry Ford

Be a Team Player

In order to be a great team, each player has to decide to be great at what he or she does for the team. To be a great team player consider the following characteristics that all great team players have in common:

- Has genuine and sincere concern for other team members.
- Takes ownership rather than blaming others
- Listens to others and is willing to consider other's point of view
- Seek to always find win/win scenarios with others on the team
- Open to constructive criticism from other team members
- Relentless resolve for results

1. Your family is your most important team. How can you be a better teammate within your family?

2. How can you become a better teammate at your place of employment?

Worry is a Poor Investment of Time

Worrying is like rocking a chair—it gives you something to do, but doesn't get you anywhere.
-Evan Esar

Stop Worrying

The late Dr. Alexis Carrel once said, "Those who do not know how to fight worry die young." Over the years, it has been noted that worry, which is synonymous with stress, has caused thousands of heart attacks, ulcers, and a myriad of other chronic illnesses. Worry is a killer, plain and simple! Its casualties include marriages, careers, finances, and health.

Suppose you were free from worry at this exact moment. What would your life look like? What would you do? What if I told you that you could rid your life of worry following three simple steps? Would you at least try them? Sure you would. Here are three simple steps to help you.

1. **Live each day each day.** This statement is just my way of saying live in "day-tight compartments". You could eliminate a great deal of worry if you just tended to today's matters instead of worrying about something that may never even come to pass. I love the scripture in the Bible (Matthew 6:34) that says, "Therefore do not worry about tomorrow, for tomorrow will worry about itself. Each day has enough trouble of its own."

2. **Invest in a journal.** Journals are a great way to vent your worries and frustrations. Simply write down every angle and detail regarding the things that are causing you to worry. After you write them down, pick out the things that you can control and place those on one side of the paper. Right next to them, list those things which you have no control over. After doing this, simply place your hand over the things you cannot control and DECIDE not to worry about them anymore. Decide to

87

focus your attention and energies on the issues that you can control. Each of us must decide not to allow worry to dominate our lives.

3. **Pray about it**. Prayer is the most effective, yet least used, weapon in each of our arsenals against worry. Prayer has the power to move mountains, and you can do it anywhere and anytime. The only requirement to tapping into the awesome power of prayer is simply to believe that God is able to handle anything that we could possibly throw his way. When you pray, use what some call the P.U.S.H. method: Pray Until Something Happens. God is always standing by just waiting for us to tap into the most powerful and potent activity in which anyone could ever partake.

The Power of Words

Words are all we have.
-Samuel Beckett

Words have power to give life, take life, enhance life, and change life because words are the very essence of life. Choose your words carefully and with compassion because you never know how your words will affect those who hear them.

You Can't Retrieve Them

That old saying, "Sticks and stones may break your bones and words will never hurt you" is a complete lie. Words do hurt and once they are said, you can't retrieve them. Sure you can apologize and seek forgiveness from the person you harmed but the damage is already done. I know people who still hurt from arguments that happened years ago but the pain of the words still sting fresh in their conscience.

An illustration that I came across teaches a good lesson on the power of our words:

A man in a small village had been found guilty of starting a malicious rumor about another man. This rumor was not only untrue, but had seriously damaged the other man's reputation and family. As is often the custom in small villages, the accused was taken before the chief of the village who served as a judge and would hear the case and decide the man's punishment if found guilty.

After hearing the facts of the case, the chief found the accused to be guilty and was now preparing to sentence the man to his punishment. The old, wise chief handed the man a large bag of feathers and told him that his only punishment would be to place a feather on the doorstep of every person to whom he had told the rumor. The man was relieved at such a light punishment and quickly took the bag of feathers and set about his task. Four hours later, the man returned to the king with the empty bag and said, "I completed your task, sir. Is there anything else?"

"Yes, the wise chief replied. Report to me in the morning and I'll give you the second half of your punishment." The man reported the next morning and was instructed that the second half of his punishment was to gather all the feathers back up and place them in the bag. "But sir," the man replied, "didn't you hear the storm that raged through our village last night? Didn't you feel the force of the winds that blew? It would be impossible to know where those feathers are now."

The wise old chief raised his index finger and pointed knowingly at the man, "Now you see, my child, the damage that you have done to another. For although you told only a few lies here and there, the storm of gossip took hold of those lies and spread them far beyond your grasp to undo them. You can regret what you said, but you can never fully undo what you've said."...

You Can Build with Them

My friend, words are all around us at all times. According to researchers, each day we average about 18,000 words because we open our mouths to speak about 700 times. With that much opening and closing of our mouths, we have and abundance of opportunities to say something to someone we wish we later could take back. The flip side is, we can find hundreds of opportunities to build someone up with our words as well.

Think about how much you enjoy receiving compliments? How often are you passing along compliments to others? How often are you building up your staff, teammates, and co-workers?

Anytime is a good time to share a word of encouragement to build someone up or to simply brighten his or her day.

Preparation is the Prerequisite of Any Great Endeavor

Unless a person has trained himself for his chance, the chance will only make him look ridiculous. A great occasion is worth to man exactly what his preparation enables him to make it.
-J.B. Matthews

There are no substitutes for solid preparation. In sports and in life, the teams and individuals who consistently perform at optimum levels are those who take the time to prepare. I had the privilege of playing college football for one of the greatest coaches of all time, Coach Tom Osborne. His ability to prepare us for upcoming games was second to none. Opposing teams probably wondered if we had obtained a copy of their playbook, because our team was seldom taken by surprise by anything that transpired on the field. Coach Osborne preached the gospel of preparation, and as a result he led his teams to the National Championship in 1994, 1995, and 1997.

What could you do right now to better prepare yourself for the life you have always wanted?

Here are a few suggestions:

1. Get a BIG GIANT UGLY GOAL. A Big Giant Ugly Goal is one in which you must plan and prepare for with all your resources; because this sucker is so big (but reachable), it's ugly!

2. Precision, Precision, Precision. You must be very precise when you're planning your life. Some people spend more time planning their grocery list than they do planning for a better and brighter future.

3. Follow through. The world is full of people who had great intentions but never followed through.

4. BE REAL. Be realistic on what you can and can't get accomplished during your day. It makes no sense to work yourself tirelessly on so many things that you accomplish none of them because it was out of your expertise or ability.

Preparation is hard work; there are no quick fixes or shortcuts when it comes to preparation but you will never regret it. It's like the old saying goes, fail to plan and you can plan to fail.

The Apostles Didn't Just Sit and Talk about the Gospel, They Took Action and Told the World about It.

No action, no results; know action, know results.
-Aaron Davis

Take Action

Las Vegas is known as the Mecca of big boxing matches. Some of the greatest fights of all time have occurred right in the desert of Las Vegas, surrounded by movie stars, bright lights radiating from the luxurious hotels, and millions of dollars awaiting the winner.

I'm about to tell you about one of the biggest fights in the history of mankind. This fight wasn't on pay-per-view. In fact, it was in the middle of nowhere. This fight didn't have any weigh-ins, where both fighters strip down to their boxers and flex their muscles and eyeball each other as they stepped on the scales. This fight took place way before there was a Muhammad Ali, Rock Marciano, or Lennox Lewis.

This fight took place several thousand years ago between two men named David and Goliath. This fight, out in the middle of a valley called Elah, didn't have any weight-class regulations. In fact, Goliath outweighed David by a few hundred pounds and was a seasoned warrior. Goliath definitely had the reach advantage over David; he was over eight feet tall. He wore 200 pounds of protective armor and equipped himself with a plethora of weapons, including a bronze javelin several inches thick, complete with a tipped twenty-five pound iron spearhead.

David, on the other hand, barely stood six feet tall and tipped the scales at about 150 pounds. David was small in stature compared to Goliath, but what he lacked in experience and equipment he more than made up for with his attitude of action. Instead of using swords, spears, and other conventional methods of combat, David went to a nearby brook and chose five smooth stones and placed them in his pouch. Once Goliath saw who had come out to challenge him, he laughed and begin talking about what he was going to do to David. As Goliath stood there talking about what he was going to do, David took immediate ACTION by running towards this massive giant.

As he ran towards Goliath, David placed a stone in his sling and launched it right at Goliath. The stone sunk into the head of Goliath, knocking him to the ground and killing him instantly.

By adopting an immediate course of action, David triumphed over the Goliath that he had to face. What about you? What giants are you facing in your life right now? Maybe it's a financial Goliath and you just can't seem to bring yourself to curb your spending habits, or perhaps you've been fired or laid off from your job. Maybe your Goliath is that you're unhappy in your current profession or position but fear the unknown. Perhaps you're dealing with a Goliath of yesterday that's preventing you from getting ahead because you're allowing the past to impede your today and tomorrow. I have some advice for you.

Take action NOW! David refused to just sit and wait for something to happen; he made things happen by taking action. All of us face Goliaths everyday, but it's those who choose to take action who become victors instead of victims.

David ran toward him. He put a rock in his sling and swung the sling around by its straps. When he let go of one strap, the rock flew out and hit Goliath on the forehead. It cracked his skull, and he fell face down on the ground. David defeated Goliath with a sling and a rock.

-1 Samuel 17:48 (CEV)

1. What Goliaths are you facing in your life today?

2. Have you really taken massive action towards defeating them or have you just allowed the Goliaths in your life to beat you day in and day out?

3. Take ACTION TODAY!!!

Rejection Opens the Door to Unlimited Possibilities

*We keep going back, stronger, not weaker, because we will not
allow rejection to beat us down. It will only strengthen our
resolve. To be successful, there is no other way.*
-Earl G. Graves

The fear of rejection causes millions of people to give up on their true
desires every day. Why does a simple two-letter word (NO) have so
much power that it causes so many to give up and settle for less? The
word "NO" has no power unless the person who hears it gives it such.
In fact, if you're in sales of any kind, your success ratio depends on the
number of rejections that you receive. Anyone in the sales profession
who hasn't grown immune to the word no had better grow immune to
having skinny kids.

In order to be a success in any area of your life, you have to come
to appreciate the rejections, knowing that the law of averages will be
on your side. The pages of history are filled with those who endured
hundreds and even thousands of rejections but pressed on and became
immortal in their respective fields. Each time you board an airplane
and climb to 30,000 feet, it's a testimony of the resolve of the famous
Wright Brothers, whose ideas were constantly rejected by others in the
aeronautics community.

If you were rejected ten times, would you keep going? How about
one hundred times? How about a thousand times? Colonel Sanders, the
founder of the world famous restaurant, Kentucky Fried Chicken, did
just that. His chicken recipe was rejected over one thousand times before he got his big break, and the rest is history.

Just imagine the type of results that you could begin to achieve if you
changed the way that you think and feel about rejection. Instead of ab-
horring the word "no" and the rejection it implies, learn to appreciate it
and move on, knowing that you're closing in on the results you desire.

1. Does the word "no" cause you to give up? What have you
   learned in the past by moving forward in spite of hearing "no"?

Gratitude Improves Your Attitude

"If one should give me a dish of sand, and tell me there were particles of iron in it, I might look for them with my eyes, and search for them with my clumsy fingers, and be unable to detect them; but let me take a magnet and sweep through it and how would it draw to itself the almost invisible particles by the mere power of attraction. The unthankful heart, like my finger in the sand, discovers no mercies; but let the thankful heart sweep through the day, and as the magnet finds the iron, so it will find, in every hour, some heavenly blessing. Only the iron in God's sand is gold!"
-Henry Ward Beecher

Gratitude is far more than just being thankful or appreciative for the things that you have. True gratitude is thankfulness in action. Gratitude is taking the time to really reflect on this gift of life.

Helps You Think Better
An attitude of gratitude helps you think well about what you have NOW instead of focusing your time on what you don't have. It's a shame that so many allow their attitude to go sour because they're so fixated on what they don't have, they cheat themselves out of the joy of being grateful for what they do have.

Gratitude is Action
I can tell my wife and kids that I love them everyday but if I fail to show that love through action then they are going to have a hard time believing that I'm truly grateful for them. True gratitude is a verb in that moves and it's active. True gratitude is showing the people in your life that you appreciate them. It's doing your best for your employer or for your own enterprise.

Gratitude is Looking Back
Can you think of a time where you survived a close call while driving? Maybe you endured a terrible illness and today your alive to tell about

it? What about an unruly son or daughter that has turned it around? Maybe you were the victim of a downsizing but your life today would not be as sweet had you not experienced that in the past? The point is that we can often look back at painful experiences that were horrible at the time, but without them we would not be who we are today. All of us can look back into our past and find plenty to be grateful for.

Each day that you're fortunate to arise in the morning try sitting up in your bed and simply deciding to be grateful for yet another day. God made no mistakes when he made you so be grateful for who you are.

Look in the Mirror: There is Your Toughest Competitor

*Thank God for competition. When our competitors upset
our plans or outdo our designs, they open infinite
possibilities of our own work to us.*
- Gil Atkinson

The world doesn't owe me, you, or anyone else anything. Everything that you acquire or accomplish will come as the direct result of your desire to do so. Of course, we all receive help from family, friends, and close advisors, who encourage us along the way. But it's up to each of us to actually put our God-given talents into action. When one begins to employ his or her talents and abilities, they immediately decide to transform from a person that's just in this race we call life, into a person that plans on making an impact in life. Only by using our talents and abilities do we differentiate ourselves from the masses. Unfortunately, many people today have no clue that they are even competing.

They refuse to hone their skills, refuse to read, and refuse to engage in on-going personal and professional development activities, such as reflective thinking, educational seminars or simply picking up a newspaper to know what's going on in the world. It's those who have no idea that they are in a race who will always finish last.

In Africa, a popular story really illustrates this point and drives it home. In the wild of Africa, the gazelle awakens to another beautiful day with only one thing on its mind: it must run faster than the fastest lion if it wishes to live another day. And each morning the lion awakens out of it's slumber knowing that it must run faster than the slowest gazelle if it wants to eat for the day. The lion knows that each day it doesn't catch the slowest gazelle is another day that it goes without eating, causing it to become weaker when chasing the gazelle the next day. The wild plains of Africa are not the only place that the game of competition and survival is played out. Whether you see yourself as the gazelle or as the lion, you had better decide to run, to compete every day, or the consequences could be deadly.

Be Different to Receive Different Results

We would worry less about what others think of us
if we realized how seldom they do.
- Ethel Barret

People don't fail; they just choose to conform to those with whom they surround themselves. Conformity is what causes many to come up short of their desires, not failure. Follow the old adage and "be yourself." You must refuse to let others design your life for you.

It Starts with You

My first three years of college were a nightmare because I chose to conform to the people that I surrounded myself with. Most of them didn't study so I didn't study. They didn't have any goals so I didn't have any goals. As I look back it's almost scary how much I became just like those I was with. After finally waking up, I made a very simple decision that rendered amazing results and changed the course of my life. I simply decided to be different. I became different in that my faith in God became the most important thing in my life. My academics became the number one priority for me during my last few years of college and my grades changed dramatically. I begin to write down my goals and study them faithfully. My life changed because I changed.

When you begin to think differently you will begin to experience different results. Every change that takes place in your life first begins with you. Individuality is what separates you from the masses; it's a shame that we often forget that we were made originals and then surrender that to be just like everyone else.

Individuality and sharp thinking is what Bill Gates used to create a billion-dollar empire, regardless of what others thought of him dropping out of college. Individuality is what made Oprah an international icon. Individuality is what Earl G. Graves, the founder and publisher of *Black Enterprises Magazine*, used to create one of the most widely circulated magazines in history. The Bible says in Psalm 139:14 "You am are fearfully and wonderfully made." We can see this in our anatomy, since no one has the same fingerprints or lines on their hands. It's evident in our DNA as it distinguishes us from anyone else.

Don't get me wrong, there are times that conformity is a good thing such as laws that govern our world and when seeking a mutual agreement on matters that bring peace rather than discord and war.

Being yourself and conforming is not an easy balance, but it's necessary. Each has its unique way of bringing stability and clarity to our sometimes-complicated world.

A last warning to those of you who truly decide to be different regardless of what others are doing or saying. You will be ridiculed! Martin Luther King, John F. Kennedy, Robert Kennedy, Medgar Evers, all refused to conform to the hatred and inequality of racism and each of them was killed as a result. These men along with thousands of others throughout our history changed the world that we live in because they were different and refused to be "just like" everyone else.

Since each of us are wonderfully made with differences that set us apart from all others, why not use our individuality to our advantage and for the betterment of mankind?

1. Have you ever abandoned whom you really are in order to fit in with a group, personally or professionally?

2. How did you feel knowing that you were selling out who you really were in order to be accepted?

3. Just be you. You can be the best you in the whole world. You can only be second when you're trying to be like someone else.

Sincerity Is a Sign of Strength

Sincerity is the highest compliment you can pay.
-Ralph Waldo Emerson

No Matter What, Be Sincere

Imagine what our world would look like if people were sincere? The courthouses and jails would be empty because those who committed crimes would be sincere in their apologies, so there would be no repeat offenders. The nuclear family would no longer be an oddity.

People would no longer have jobs but would have careers, because they would be sincere with respect to their own career desires. Stereotyping would be a thing of the past, because people would sincerely seek to know one another rather than casting them into a one-size-fits all molds.

World hunger would end, because the world would make sincere efforts to fight the monster of starvation and AIDS with action rather than mere fiery speeches and empty promises. Human relations would take on a whole new meaning if we allowed sincerity to pervade each area of our lives. A dream? Maybe. A possibility? Absolutely.

Serving Others Improves Your Life

Find out how much God has given you and from it, take
what you need; the remainder is needed by others.
-St. Augustine

Today's society classifies people as successful if they have amassed large fortunes, are heads of major corporations, have physical beauty, and know the right people. All of these things are nice and there is absolutely nothing wrong attaining these. But, I choose to define greatness according to a different source: the Bible. Contrary to popular belief, the Bible says that the greatest among us will be our servants. Wow! You may be reading this saying, "Serving? Yeah right!" It's no misprint, though. Serving others is what makes anyone truly great!

Let's have a closer look at this. Take sales, for example. Those who are truly successful in sales are the men and women who seek to serve their client's need and objectives. Isn't this serving? What about the great politicians and business magnates of times past? McDonalds has served billions and billions because of their outstanding service. Sam Walton, the founder of the billion-dollar Wal Mart empire, believed that if you give customers a great product for a great price and offered service with a smile, then you could make a pretty good living. I think his philosophy has some merit to it, don't you?

The neighborhood watch in your local community is a service; the Sunday school teacher who taught you the books of the Bible was performing a service; the missionaries all over the world are great examples of true altruistic service. To give real service you must truly value and appreciate those whom you seek to serve.

1. How could you be a better servant personally and professionally?

2. How does serving others make you feel? How do you feel when you are being served?

The Most Important People You Can Honor are Your Parents

We never know the love of the parent until
we become parents ourselves.
-Henry Ward Beecher

Thank God for Your Myles and Martha

The words on this page could never express the love, appreciation, and respect that I have for my parents. Myles and Martha Davis taught me that I could do whatever I set my mind to, provided that I kept my faith in God. Even as a young boy running around our dirt covered yard (with six kids, grass was a foreign object), my parents instilled in me the value of integrity, hard work, and independence from all but God.

The lessons that I learned at our dinner table have formed the bedrock of who and what I am today. I am definitely not perfect (my wife Brooke will tell you that), but I try daily to be all that God would have me be. I learned the value of traveling the road less traveled from my father, Myles Davis, long before I read the famous ***"Road Less Traveled"*** poem by Robert Frost.

My father was the quintessential man who took the road less traveled. In 1963, he moved his family to a predominantly white Lincoln, Nebraska, in search of a safer environment as to escape the unforgiving and mean streets of Pittsburgh, Pennsylvania. It was from my Dad that I learned the value of hard work, never depending on any program or system to determine how far I could go in life. My dad is a man of few words who always wears a smile that could shatter any obstacle that stands in his path because he lives his life by the passage found in Nehemiah 8:10, "The joy of the Lord is your strength."

I learned grit and determination from a lady that stands barely five foot two inches tall (but we all know that dynamite comes in small packages). My mom would never allow me to hang my head after a poor performance on the field or in the classroom. She would encourage us to learn from it but wouldn't ever allow our heads to drop in defeat no matter what the score or grade was. She instilled in me that each of us has the final say on the score if we only keep pressing ahead.

My parents are the reason that I am who I am today, and I thank God daily that I was given the chance to grow up in a home where both of my parents were active in my life.

Mom and Dad, I love you and cherish you for all that you planted in my heart and mind. Your example of faith, love and discipline has equipped me as a husband, father and businessman and I'm eternally grateful to both of you. I love you dearly!

One Final Truth

Words of true wisdom are as refreshing as bubbling brook.
-Proverbs 18:4

Every book is a miracle once completed, and this one is no exception. I'm well aware that this book is not Pulitzer prize material for excellence in writing, but hopefully the timeless wisdom found within the pages of this book have refreshed every area of your life.

If there happens to be shortcomings in this book, they are strictly my own; whatever value comes from this work I owe to family, friends, life and, most importantly, my best friend, Jesus Christ!

Each day is precious and impossible to retrieve once it's gone. With that in mind, pour all of yourself passionately and patiently into each day, because each day is all you really have.

Get Aaron Davis's **FREE Inspirational Moment E-Newsletter** going to www.aarondavisspeaks.com

To have Aaron Davis give your audience an **experience**, not just **another talk**, contact AARON DAVIS PRESENTATIONS, INC. AT:

1.800.474.8755

Email: adavis@aarondavisspeaks.com

On the Web: www.aarondavisspeaks.com